MURDER BY METHANOL

MURDER BY METHANOL

and other tales from the world of kidneys

---

by

Jerry Posen, MD

Copyright © 2014 by Gerald A. Posen

All rights reserved. This book or any portion thereof may not be reproduced or used in any manner whatsoever without the express written permission of the publisher except in the case of uses permitted by copyright law.

ISBN-13: 978-1-312-68918-3

Published by:
Lulu Press, Inc.
3101 Hillsborough St.
Raleigh, NC 27607
www.lulu.com

First printing, 2014
Printed in the United States of America

This book is dedicated to all of the patients who have allowed me to be part of their lives; to all the hospital and clinic support staff who helped make the hospital and clinics function as well as they do; to my students and residents who taught me as I tried to teach them; to the nurses, without whose support and dedication none of this would be possible; to my sons, who often wondered where their father was on weekends, and when I was there to what great adventures we had; and, finally, to my precious beloved wife Josée, without whom much of this would not have transpired. She stood by me and supported me through all my ups and downs. She is a great editor to whom I owe all my final copies of articles, reports, and important letters.

Contents

The kidney	xi
Prologue	xiii
Smarter than the teacher	1
The best medicine	11
Life and death	17
The Yogi Bear fan club	31
Murder by methanol	51
North by northwest	61
In the lab	67
The dog that couldn't pee	71
Something in the water	77
Locked up	85
The heart of the matter	91
Fighting panic	97
Haemodialysis	101
Statistics and more statistics	115
Suing the minister of health	121
Nimkee	131
Out of Africa	139

New developments	147
In from the cold	155
Kidney stones	159
At the scene	165
A walk down memory lane	169
Envoi	177

I have spent forty-two years intimately involved with kidney disease. I was fortunate enough to be a part of a team doing the first chronic haemodialysis in Canada, the first home haemodialysis in Canada, early kidney transplant, and early peritoneal dialysis. Many interesting things have happened to me over the course of my career. My students and colleagues have often remarked at their interest in these stories and have suggested I write them down.

This book is a series of stories of my becoming a doctor and my career in nephrology.

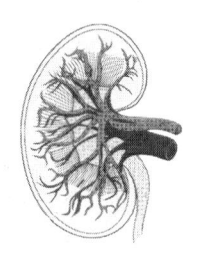

The kidney

The kidneys, as with many organs in the body, are essential for survival. They act to maintain the body's fluid and electrolyte balance. If we ingest too much fluid, the kidney excretes the excess. If we lose fluids or don't drink enough, the kidney preserves the status by putting out less urine. By the same token, if we take in too much salt or other similar electrolytes the kidney either retains the electrolytes or excretes them according to the body's needs. Everything that we take in by mouth is either excreted in the stool or absorbed and metabolized by the body. But many of the products of metabolism are toxic to many systems of the body (such as neurologic, musculoskeletal, and gastric). The kidneys eliminate these toxic products through the urine. The kidneys also adjust the blood pressure and level of red blood cells. People that develop kidney disease retain toxins, have trouble passing urine, have anaemia, high blood pressure, and bone disease. All of this leads to gradual deterioration of the body and general unwellness, and if untreated will eventually lead to death.

The commonest causes of kidney failure are arteriosclerosis (similar to that causing heart disease), diabetes, and high blood pressure.

People with kidney problems may feel normal until the kidney function has been reduced to less than 15 percent. That is why when a patient receives a kidney transplant they only require one normally functioning kidney.

The artificial kidney, or dialysis, can remove the body's toxins and adjust its fluids. We can then keep the patients relatively well by controlling the blood pressure, improving their anaemia, and preventing bone disease with the use of medication.

Prologue

Once, as I was driving home from work in Ottawa, a motorcycle in front of me spun out of control and hit a car. I pulled my own car over immediately and ran to assess the situation. The cyclist, bleeding and barely conscious, had lost the lower part of one of his legs from the knee down.

I quickly stabilized him and got the bleeding under control, and then I had a passerby hold his neck while I went searching for the severed leg. I found it some distance away, covered with dirt and blood. Carefully, I wrapped the limb in a blanket I had in the trunk of my car and returned to tend to the cyclist. When the ambulance came I gave the leg to the attendants and instructed them to give it to the hospital physicians.

At the hospital, the doctors were able to sew the leg back on. The motorcyclist made a full recovery and was able to walk – and bike – again.

MURDER BY METHANOL

and other tales from the world of kidneys

Smarter than the teacher

I was born Gerald Allan Posen in 1935 in Toronto, the son of David Posen and Faye Boigon. I grew up in Toronto during the war years, indistinguishable from any other Jewish boy growing up at that time. My mother used to tell the story of how, as a third-grader at Lansdowne Elementary School, I arrived home every day clutching a note from my long-suffering teacher.

Finally, my parents went in for the *big meeting* where my teacher told them, "Jerry is always arguing with me. It's as if he thinks he knows more than I do!"

Needless to say, my parents were upset. As soon as they returned home, they sat me down at the dining room table and, in the presence of the usual assortment of aunts and uncles who always happened to be by, demanded an explanation.

"It's simple," I said, precocious even then. "I don't just think I know more than she does. I do."

And I did!

* * *

My uncle, Dr. Melvin Boigon, was my role model and the impetus behind my decision to study medicine. He was my mother's youngest sibling, the only boy in a family of six girls, and just fifteen years older than I. In many ways he was like a brother to me and, being Canadian-born, he was much more in sync with my generation.

After he graduated from medical school, my uncle went to New York for postgraduate studies in psychiatry. There he met and married another psychiatric resident, Helen Wasserman, a very special woman who became my aunt. She was quite beautiful and very smart. That aunt also played a role in my decision to pursue medicine. It happened at a family gathering.

Like most immigrant families our family was very close. The whole clan always got together for bar mitzvahs, weddings, and funerals. Everyone came. It was at one such gathering that my aunt was able to resolve a heartbreaking situation. My cousin Howard, the firstborn grandson of my grandfather's brother, was gravely ill. The child, just three years old, was wasting away and close to death. Although my aunt was a psychiatrist, she always kept up with the latest medical literature and because of this the child's life was saved. In a recent issue of the *New England Journal of Medicine* she had read about a New York physician who had discovered that Celiac disease was caused by a severe allergy to wheat germ. By simply eliminating wheat germ from the diet, this doctor contended, an individual could lead a normal life. My aunt strongly suspected this was Howard's problem and arranged for him to go to New York immediately to be seen by the doctor. After undergoing many tests, he was diagnosed with Celiac disease and began a therapy that consisted of a diet completely free of wheat flour. The little boy who had been close to death thrived. He is now a very successful lawyer in Denver, Colorado.

I had already felt that I wanted to become a doctor; seeing this medical miracle at the age of sixteen put the final stamp on it.

* * *

I was always an average student. As I went through Forest Hill Village High School, I began to feel that I'd have to give up my dream of becoming a doctor because I probably wasn't smart enough to get into medical school. The kids who got the highest grades always boasted about how little, if any, studying or homework they did. Like them, I also did little, if any, studying or homework but, unlike them, my grades kept falling until I failed grade twelve English and French.

At that time, Ontario high schools comprised five grades – nine through thirteen – and in order to graduate from grade thirteen you had to accumulate nine credits. That is, you had to pass nine grade thirteen courses. I decided to drop French, which I figured I had little or no chance of passing, but dropping English was not an option. English was compulsory and, because I was repeating English, I could only do six additional courses that year, which meant I had no choice but to spend an extra year in high school.

I made up my mind to show the teachers that I wasn't stupid after all. For the next two years, I studied hard and did all my homework. By the end of the second year, I had taken all the required courses. In fact, I'd taken a total of twelve courses – three more than the nine required to graduate. I got eleven A grades and one B. The B was in English grammar. But I got an A in English literature. And I discovered how much I loved the sciences: chemistry, physics, and biology.

I also learned two very important lessons in those two years of grade thirteen. First, if I studied hard enough I could get good grades and, second, the kids who boasted that they never studied or did their homework were lying. By buckling down and really digging in, my dream of studying medicine became a reality.

*   *   *

In 1955, I was accepted into the two-year premed program at the University of Western Ontario.

Western's premed program was very well designed. It was based on the philosophy *forget high school – show us what you can do in university* and, to that end, every course we took was geared to learning, understanding, and applying medical ethics. For example, our English lit curriculum included *King Lear*, Sinclair Lewis's *Arrowsmith*, and *The Brothers Karamazov*. Each of these novels contains a medical situation or situations that always led to in-depth class discussions on medical ethics. The same was true of the foci of our psychology and philosophy courses. We did not have to strain to reach the ethical conclusions in those courses.

Our workload was very heavy; classes and labs daily from 8:00 AM to 5:00 PM and frequent tests and essay assignments. We all worried about getting the grades because we knew that being accepted into the premed program was no guarantee of being accepted into the medical school. Anyone who graduated from grade thirteen with the required nine credits had a very good chance of getting into the premed program, but in order to move into second-year premed you had to attain a minimum C+ average, with no failures. And then, to be accepted into medical school, you had to have completed the two-year premed course with an overall B+ average. While a B+ average may not sound like much, the marking was more rigorous then and a B was similar to an A– today.

My premed class started out with seventy hopefuls; only thirty or so made it into medical school. We were warned from day one in premed that the cut would be drastic, and it was. But given my success in the final two years of high school, I felt confident that with hard work I would make it. I was right. In fact, in my second year, I had an A average and made the Dean's List.

That same year I also discovered I could have fun and still get good grades. It was simply a matter of organizing my time so that I always did the necessary amount of studying, then used the free time I had for serious play. That was a major life lesson.

In those years there were courses in chemistry, physics, physical chemistry, botany, zoology, and mathematics (specifically calculus), as well as a very intense course in statistics.

I learned another valuable life lesson from the statistics course. I was so comfortable with statistics that the night before the exam I gave a tutorial at our fraternity house for about ten of my classmates. The next day I strode into the examination brimming with confidence, fully expecting to attain a perfect mark of one hundred. But then, in the first of the ten exam questions, I made an arithmetic error. I knew my answer was off but instead of just accepting it and getting maybe eight or nine marks out of the possible ten, I persisted until I found the error and corrected it. There were no calculators then; mathematics was very involved and had to be done mentally and figured out on paper. By the time I caught the mistake I didn't have sufficient time to complete all ten questions. I ended up with a B, while my tutorial students all got A and B+ grades! That experience taught me not to be such a perfectionist.

* * *

Years later, when I was a resident in nephrology at McGill University, one of my first consults came from Dr. John Girvin in neurosurgery. John had graduated from Western about three years ahead of me. He'd been an excellent student and always stood at or near the top of his class. He was also captain and first-string end on the intercollegiate football team and centre and captain of the intercollegiate basketball team. I couldn't believe that he was asking for my opinion. Fortunately, I knew my field and helped him with his case. It turned out well and we became friends. He was clever but not a genius, just extremely well-rounded.

One day I asked John how he had managed to do all the things he did and still maintain his marks. He explained that, in his student days, the sports teams traveled to games by train and, while all the others were fooling around en route, he was studying. He applied the same rule for between-game practices. "No matter what," he told me, "I tried to get in two hours of intense study a night." John became a very successful neurosurgeon in London, Ontario, as well as a full professor and head of the division of neurosurgery at the University of Western Ontario. I've used his story on many occasions as an example for my medical students. One has to be organized. Once you are, you find the time first for school and then for play.

My final year of medical school was my best academically and that year I played on three hockey teams and did many other activities as well.

* * *

When I first arrived at medical school in 1957, I was very excited at the prospect of studying bacteriology. I'd always liked medical history: the story of Semmelweis and childbirth fever; Pasteur and rabies; the plague; the great influenza pandemic of 1918; the changes antibiotics brought to medicine. All of it fascinated me and I was looking forward to this course more than any other.

I was very disappointed, then, when I discovered that it was taught in the most boring manner possible. The principal focus was on classifications – all taxonomy and memory work. No attempt was made to introduce the important related history and nothing of clinical relevance was ever brought up. I stopped going to class, studied from the textbook, and still got a B.

In the first and second years we also did a course in biochemistry and physiology. This combined the study of the chemical basis of the body and the functioning of all the organs. It was very complex, and the most difficult part involved the kidneys. I loved it. I knew then that I wanted to learn more about the kidneys and kidney disease. But there were two problems: one, no matter how hard I studied I always got a B+ – never an A – and, two, at that time there was no treatment for kidney failure and many young people died of kidney disease. As you will see, I lucked into the early treatment of kidney failure at the end of my internship.

* * *

At the end of my first and second years of medical school I had a summer job doing research in the department of medical physics, a one-person department headed by a Dr. Alan Burton.

Dr. Burton was a most interesting gentleman. During the Second World War he had studied the body's reaction to cold by immersing medical students in cold baths while trying various items of clothing on them and measuring temperature response.

His research showed that it is the head that loses heat fastest, which resulted in a different helmet design for fighter pilots. In 2010, he was inducted into the Canadian Medical Hall of Fame for his work in protecting the body from cold.

In addition to one of my classmates and me, Dr. Burton had two graduate students working with him. One was an escapee from the USSR who told unbelievable stories about the Stalinist regime. Every one of them turned out to be true: the gulags in Siberia, the purges and executions, the total control by the state. I believed him, but some dismissed his stories as bogus.

The other graduate student was a brilliant woman, a wonderful researcher who became head of the department when Dr. Burton stepped down.

Every morning Dr. Burton came in at around 9:30 and called a halt to all work. Then he, the two graduate students, my classmate, and I would sit around an oval table drinking coffee and talking. The discussion might centre on a scientific or political subject or just be a mental exercise, such as why the world didn't talk in Esperanto. We'd all contribute to the discussion and we often sat around talking for an hour or two. It was a wonderful learning experience.

Over the two summers I spent in the lab, my project was to prove that the way we measured blood pressure – which, incidentally, is the method still used – gave incorrect intermediate results, but involved two errors that cancelled each other out, such that the final number was correct. I designed a system with Dr. Burton that, over both summers, I could not get to work right. Meanwhile, my classmate was designing and building a special cage for rats in order to measure the temperature in a rat's tail. I don't think either of us changed or contributed to the world of science, but we both learned a great deal about the scientific method and many other things. This project also sparked my life long interest in high blood pressure.

(In retrospect, I realize that Dr. Burton hired us to teach us about being scientists and to give us good paying summer jobs, which we needed, rather than to conduct earth-shaking medical research.)

The best medicine

I considered myself very fortunate to do my internship at the Montreal General Hospital. In our group of forty-eight interns, ten had stood first in their respective medical school classes, out of thirteen medical schools in Canada. Many of the house staff went on to become professors, heads of departments, and deans of medical schools across Canada.

One of our number was Phil Gold, who later became famous. Phil went on to do some very exciting research on cancer, won a Gairdner Award, was featured on the cover of *Life* magazine, and was inducted into the Canadian Medical Hall of Fame. He ultimately became a professor of medicine and then head of medicine at McGill. Phil was also a close friend and godfather to my eldest son.

But in 1961, we were young interns together and there were many duties we interns hadn't been told about. I guess we were expected to know instinctively what was required of us, as the following tale will illustrate.

One night, shortly after we began our internship, Phil was on call covering wards for interns off duty that night. He was awakened at about 3:00 AM by a nurse who told him that a Mr. X (who was not one of his patients) had ceased to breathe.

"Is he dead?" Phil mumbled into the phone.

"Yes," the nurse replied. "He's dead."

"I'm sorry to hear it," Phil mumbled again. "Thanks for letting me know. Goodnight."

He hung up the phone and immediately fell back into a deep sleep.

Within moments the phone rang again and the same nurse repeated the same message.

"Mr. X has ceased breathing," she said. "He is dead." Once again Phil offered his condolences and said goodnight.

The third phone call came from the night supervisor.

"Dr. Gold," she said sternly, "you have to pronounce the patient dead."

Again Phil asked, "Is he dead?"

The supervisor replied, "Yes."

Phil said, "I now pronounce Mr. X dead. Goodnight." And he hung up.

The fourth and final phone call came from a senior resident demanding that Dr. Gold go to the ward in person and officially pronounce the patient dead. This time Phil understood. He leapt out of bed, went to ward in person, pronounced the patient dead, came back, and went to sleep.

* * *

During my surgical rotation at MGH, I had the great good fortune to be working with the chief of surgery, Dr. H. Rocke Robertson. Dr. Robertson and I got along very well and one day he demonstrated his faith in me by asking if I would do a sigmoidoscopic examination (that is, inserting a tube into the rectum, inspecting, and ruling out a tumour) on a patient.

The gentleman was a personal patient of the chief's, an important businessman and a major donor to the hospital. Dr. Robertson explained that he had to attend a special reception in the hospital with all sorts of distinguished guests but assured me he would be available if I needed him.

The procedure was one I had done under Dr. Robertson's supervision several times, so I was supremely confident that I could handle the assignment and claim bragging rights after the fact. I did the procedure as required: I put the scope in, then, as one normally does, tried to remove the end. That was when all hell broke loose. The end of the scope snapped off. Try as I might, I could not get it out. I wasn't confident now – I was beside myself. I had to bite the bullet, find the reception room, find Dr. Robertson and tell him that his patient had half a sigmoidoscope stuck in his rectum that I couldn't get out.

The chief took the news calmly, like the professional he was. He swiftly arranged for a general anesthetic in the operating room and for a fellow surgeon, the very competent Dr. Fraser Gurd, to remove the offending article. In no time flat the scope was out and the patient was fine. Dr. Robertson explained to him that the fault lay with the scope and that no damage had been done.

Dr. Robertson continued to work closely with me and never said another word about the incident. He was an exemplary surgeon, teacher, and researcher. He went on to become head of McGill University's department of surgery and ultimately principal and vice-chancellor of the university.

* * *

Paramedic service had not yet been developed when I was interning at MGH, so every time an ambulance went out an emergency ward intern had to go with it.

Emergency ward interns were assigned to be on ambulance call every third day. When it was your turn someone else took over for you in the ER. We all looked forward to being the ambulance doctor because often what we were doing in the ER wasn't very exciting. One friend on ambulance call got to deliver a baby on two separate occasions.

Two weeks passed before I got the big call: "Dr. Posen to the ambulance!" I was very excited when it came. I put on a fresh white coat, straightened my stethoscope, and away I went. I sat in the right front seat and, with sirens blazing, we sped through Montreal traffic.

We arrived at the address, a typical Montreal-style upper and lower two-family flat. A long outside staircase led to the second-floor lodgings. A large group of people had assembled on the sidewalk and, when I stepped out of the ambulance, a collective sigh of relief went up: "The doctor's here! The doctor's here!" they said to each other. "Hurray!"

The hero had arrived.

I stood very straight and, in an attempt to appear terribly professional, I assumed a very serious expression. The scene was set. I started to run up that long, long staircase … only to trip on the top step and tumble all the way down. The crowd was speechless and so was I. I felt utterly foolish. I learned a lesson in humility that day.

As it turned out, the patient was not seriously ill and there really had been no need for a doctor with the ambulance. Nevertheless, we were obliged to take the patient to our hospital, where I took over responsibility for her.

I went out with the ambulance many times after that first experience and the only time I was useful was when a large tire had fallen on a man. He was in excruciating pain so I gave him morphine IV, a large dose, but it did nothing. I repeated with a larger dose, and still nothing. I then gave him an even larger dose and this time it worked.

I was always frightened to give too much morphine because I knew how dangerous the drug was. This experience taught me a lesson in pain control: give the drug until the pain is relieved!

* * *

Between 1967 and 1974, when I was working at the Ottawa General Hospital, the OGH was using ultra-filtration, a way of getting rid of excess fluid in the body without dialyzing. This type of dialysis didn't need extra blood and could be achieved by a patient's blood pressure alone. However, it presented a huge problem because the entire process was done without blood pumps; even our acute renal failure patients were dialyzed without blood pumps.

On one occasion we had a patient in the intensive care unit who must have had a forty- to fifty-kilogram fluid overload. His heart was obviously very strong because it was the only thing working in him. He was so unbelievably overloaded with fluid that he looked a ringer for Popeye. We had to get the excess fluid out of him before the strain on his heart would cause heart failure and death.

The correct way to remove fluid is by pulling it out through the dialyzer. This process is called negative pressure, or suction. Today, a pump does it. At that time, however, we didn't have a pump. Fortunately, I remembered from my university physics course that suction increases by increasing the length of the tube to the ground. In my infinite wisdom, I decided the best way to handle the situation was to hang the tube from the dialysate out the window and let it drain, instead of having it go to the usual drain on the hospital room floor. The longer the tube, the more negative pressure we got, so I hung the tube way, way out the window, thus creating a massive amount of suction.

It worked!

I succeeded in taking most of the fluid off this patient and, as the treatment progressed, he started feeling better. Within four hours he was almost back to normal and we let his kidneys do the rest.

Unbeknownst to me, however, the liquid from the tube was running onto the roof of the chapel that was attached to the hospital. It began to leak through the roof and into the chapel! The good nuns were certain that the "rain" they were witnessing was a sign from God, for outside the sun was shining brightly. They didn't know – and I never disillusioned them of the fact – that this "rain" was actually a type of urine flowing not from God but from the intensive care unit.

The roof was eventually repaired.

Life and death

In the summer of 1962, I took a job as a locum in Espanola, a small town in northern Ontario. The doctors had left; I would be on my own for the duration. Sudbury, the closest city, was about an hour and a half away.

One day a young woman of about eighteen came into the emergency room of the local hospital with her mother. The daughter, a big woman about five feet ten inches tall and generally broad, was clutching her abdomen and complaining of severe abdominal pain. Her mother said she thought it might be gall bladder disease or perhaps something she had eaten. Whatever it was, she was obviously in terrible distress.

After reassuring Mother that I would look after her daughter, I took her into the examining room where I asked her about the pain. She described it as very severe cramps that sometimes went into her back. The pain had started a couple of hours earlier and didn't seem traceable to any food she ate. She didn't volunteer much more information.

I asked her to lie down and, on examination, I discovered the pain was because she was in labour. She had a large uterus, which wasn't obvious from just looking at her, but there was no question that Daughter was in quite active labour. We rushed her to the delivery suite where I delivered her of a healthy seven-pound baby.

When I told Mother that her daughter's abdominal pain had been a pregnancy, she couldn't believe it. She was adamant that her daughter had never had a relationship with a male. Daughter agreed entirely that this was the case. I left it to Daughter to explain the virgin birth to her mother, who was suddenly the grandmother of a bouncing baby girl.

* * *

In Espanola I became friendly with a priest who was in charge of a summer camp for underprivileged boys from Toronto. The camp was situated on Manitoulin Island some twenty miles from town and since there wasn't a doctor on site, the priest brought his medical problems in to see me. He also invited me to the camp for supper several times where we'd have interesting discussions on religion and politics.

Late one evening I received an emergency call to get to the camp as quickly as possible. I hopped into my sports car and took off like a bat out of hell, traveling as fast as I could along the narrow, winding road that led to the camp. I didn't know what awaited me but I had a feeling it wasn't anything good. When I arrived, I was spirited to the waterfront where there lay the body of an eleven-year-old boy. He'd gone missing after supper and they'd found him on the shore. I realized upon seeing him that he was no longer alive, and had not been for a while. I got down and examined him and pronounced him dead. It was an extremely difficult situation. I knew the camp was very careful with its young charges and took great pride in running a first-rate facility for these underprivileged kids. It looked accidental to me but I never knew whether that was the case or whether he had drowned himself, because my month in Espanola was up.

What happened was a tragedy that could happen anywhere. One feels so sad and helpless in such a situation. I always hoped the camp was able to continue.

* * *

In 1960, my final year as a medical student, I did my obstetrics rotation at St. Joseph's, a large Catholic hospital in London where many of the general practitioners did their own deliveries. Ultrasound for diagnosis had not been invented at that time.

One day a husband and wife arrived at the hospital. The wife, a large woman, was in labour. The couple already had three children, all boys. This would be their fourth child and they were hoping desperately for a girl.

The woman's GP was a fine doctor and a very nice person. We'd worked together before so he said to me, "Jerry, why don't you deliver this lady. I'll stand back and watch you." I delivered the baby and all went well. It was healthy but small, only about three-and-a-half pounds, yet the mother's abdomen was still very large.

The GP furrowed his brow and said, "Something else must be going on here." He examined the patient and found another baby! It was in breech position – that is, bottom, rather than head, first. He delivered baby number two, which was approximately the same size as baby number one, three pounds. This baby was fine too, but the patient's abdomen was still too big.

The GP looked at me and said, "I'd better check again." When he checked, he discovered there was yet another baby in there! Baby number three was also a breech birth, which he delivered quite easily. The mother's abdomen was much smaller now. We were quite pleased with ourselves because we had just delivered, between the two of us, triplets: three small but quite healthy boys.

Now it was time to go out to speak to the husband who was waiting for news that he had a baby girl. When we told him he was the lucky father of three healthy boys he turned pale and couldn't talk for a few moments. I don't think they ever thanked us for the delivery.

The babies all did fine and so did the parents.

* * *

That final year of medical school, I did a rotation in the pediatrics ward at the Children's Hospital in London. On my very first night on call, I was telephoned and asked to admit a four-year-old with acute leukemia. I went directly to the hospital and got out the patient's old chart. Going over it, I realized this child was very sick and would die soon. At that time there was no therapy for leukemia.

I'd left the door to the office open and, as I stood reading the chart, a little guy who looked reasonably well came in and I started playing with him. We did various silly things for about half an hour with the two of us laughing very hard and working up a sweat. Then his parents appeared to say his room was ready and they took him off.

I finished my chart review and went to the ward. The nurse led me into a room where I discovered my little friend waiting to be admitted. I tried to act normal but I was devastated.

When I left that little guy I knew that I couldn't do pediatrics. I loved kids but I got too involved with them and too emotional. I really admire my pediatric colleagues; they can be cheerful and effective and not become emotionally involved with the little people. Most of the time I'm able to remain detached from older people because they understand what's happening. But, as you will see, there was one time in my internship – during my medical rotation in August, 1961 – when I was not able to remain detached.

* * *

On another pediatrics rotation, when I was at the Montreal Children's Hospital covering the newborn ICU, I received instructions to accompany the ambulance to pick up a premature baby from a smaller hospital and bring him to the Children's. The infant was very tiny; he weighed maybe two pounds. He was in an incubator and he did not look good.

During the drive the baby's heart stopped. I took the infant in my arms, blew gently into his mouth, and gave closed cardiac massage with my thumb. I cried and I prayed, but it was not to be. The baby survived just to the ICU but died very quickly after.

* * *

Sometime in 1971, when I was working in Ottawa, eight-year-old David Lafrance was admitted to the hospital with haemolytic uremic syndrome, also known as hamburger disease. David had been camping with his parents, and had eaten an undercooked hamburger that contained *E. coli* bacteria. He quickly developed severe anemia and acute renal failure.

Dr. Norman Wolfish, a personal friend of mine, was a pediatric nephrologist at the Ottawa General Hospital. Young David belonged in his care. David's kidneys didn't improve and it was certain he needed chronic haemodialysis two to three times a week for life or until he had a successful transplant. However,

Norman had done only acute haemodialysis and this patient required chronic dialysis.

I convinced Norman that he was a very smart physician and could learn how to manage a patient on chronic haemodialysis. I'd teach him what he needed to know and be there whenever he needed help. The Children's Hospital of Eastern Ontario (CHEO) was not yet built and the only option was to send the child to the Hospital for Sick Children in Toronto. This was not a desirable alternative because, if the young lad had to be dialyzed chronically in Toronto, his parents would have a tough time managing their other children and their jobs.

We decided we could do it in Ottawa and, as I knew he would, Norman learned the technique and eventually went on to set up a very good total pediatric nephrology unit in Ottawa. David is still alive and reasonably well on his fifth transplant.

Norman Wolfish and I go back a long way. Our parents were friends who often double-dated before they were married in 1928, and my sister married Norman's first cousin. After I graduated from UWO Medical School and Norman graduated from University of Toronto Medical School, we both opted for nephrology, I at McGill, Norman at New York University. He also did pediatrics in New York and, in fact, had planned to remain there. We hadn't talked since high school. Then, one day in March, 1970, I was in my office at the Ottawa General Hospital when I heard a familiar sounding voice in the hall. I got up from my chair, looked in the corridor, and there was Norman with the chief of pediatrics. He had seen the *Dr. Posen* sign on my door and wondered if it was the same Jerry Posen. Indeed it was and we were delighted to see each other.

Norman explained that he was living in New York but was looking for a position in Canada because of his Vietnam War draft eligibility – the same reason, as you will see, that prompted my own departure from New York in 1969. The chief of pediatrics wasn't looking for a new staff man at the time but I spoke to the chief of nephrology, Dr. George Jaworski, and convinced him that Norman would be a good addition to the university and the hospital. George then convinced the chief of pediatrics to offer him a job. It was agreed that he could start in July.

But two weeks after he returned to New York, Norman realized he had to hightail it out of the country, and fast, because if he received a draft notice while living in the US he'd have to serve, or be considered a draft dodger – with all that that entailed. The hospital and university agreed to let him start immediately.

Norman came to Ottawa and moved in with us. Two weeks later his wife, Elaine, and their two children (they later added a third) arrived and lived with us for a couple of weeks until they found a townhouse to move into. We remain friends to this day.

* * *

In 1976, the only two CHEO pediatric nephrologists, Dr. Wolfish and Dr. Peter MacLean, asked if I would cover them for a weekend. Norman and Peter assured me that weekends were quiet. "Nothing ever happens," they said. "We just need a name that people can call in the unlikely event a problem arises." Since I was already on call at the Civic Hospital that weekend, I figured I could easily handle being on call at the Children's Hospital as well.

It turned out I could, but not easily.

On Friday evening, I received a call that a three-month-old baby was in renal failure and desperately sick. It had been many, many years since I'd looked at the fluids or drugs used for treating babies and, as I raced to CHEO, I was very nervous, to say the least.

I examined the infant, determined that she had pyelonephritis, was dehydrated, and was in renal failure. I treated her along with a superb team at CHEO's ICU. Fortunately, she responded to fluids, electrolytes, and the proper antibiotics, so she didn't need dialyzing. Between consulting medical books on what doses of the drugs to use to treat an infant pediatric patient, keeping close watch on the little one, and running back and forth between the Civic and the Children's, I was quite stressed. Happily, she made it through the weekend and on Monday morning Drs. Wolfish and MacLean returned and took over her treatment.

But the tale does not end there.

Fast forward to 1994, when I received the referral of a young lady, a university student who had been followed by CHEO but now was eighteen and no longer eligible for treatment there. Although she was essentially well, she was being followed for reflux because of problems she'd had as a baby and for which she'd required surgery.

As I went over her history, I realized this young lady was the very baby I had worked on so diligently that long-ago weekend in 1976. When I told her the story of how I had treated her as an infant in crisis, we hugged and cried. I was very gratified to see how well she had progressed.

Meeting her after all those years and seeing how she had thrived was worth all the grey hair.

* * *

One evening I received a call from a physician at another Ottawa hospital whose patient was dying of renal failure. The patient had a very high potassium level, which, if left untreated, would cause heart stoppage and death.

The physician wasn't aware that haemodialysis, especially chronic haemodialysis, was being done in Ottawa. But, at the time, we were treating about twenty patients on a regular regime of eight-hour sessions three times per week and they were doing very well. I advised him what he should do before sending the patient by ambulance to our hospital where I would see him in emergency.

The patient was an immigrant from China in his forties. He had recently brought his wife, three daughters, and his mother to Ottawa. A year before, he'd opened a restaurant on Montreal Road in Ottawa (The Dragon) that, due to hard work, was doing very well.

When the patient arrived at the hospital with his terrified family, only he could speak English. The family was sure the father was going to die. I went over him and realized he was in renal failure. He needed immediate dialysis. I was also quite confident that it would not be a problem to treat him and start chronic haemodialysis. I had him admitted to the ICU and quickly started therapy. Everything went well. Within an hour he began to wake up.

Ordinarily, I would have gone home and left the ICU staff and residents to follow him during the night but, just as I was getting ready to leave, I received a call from a physician in Cornwall. He had an eighteen-year-old girl with a septic abortion, whose blood pressure was falling. She'd stopped putting out urine and her potassium was in the dangerous range. I instructed the doctor to start therapy to control her potassium which, if left untreated, would kill her quickly, and send her by ambulance to the General emergency.

I arranged for the young woman to be sent up to the ICU. I examined her and found that her uterus was infected from a knitting needle attempt at an abortion. Her blood pressure was unstable – in fact, very low – and her potassium was climbing. There was no time for dialysis to treat the high potassium so I treated it with intravenous drugs and adjusted the medication while watching the heart on a running electrocardiogram. I knew this solution was temporary and that she needed an immediate hysterectomy, the only way to save her life.

Her blood pressure was so low and her pulse so fast that the anesthesiologist and the surgeon were reluctant to do anything until I stabilized her. I convinced them to operate even without much of a blood pressure and I watched the electrocardiogram on a monitor in the operating room, treating the elevated potassium as necessary during the operation. The anesthetic was keeping the patient asleep, I was keeping her alive. As soon as the surgeon clamped the uterine veins her blood pressure came up.

We moved her back to the ICU, placed her bed beside that of my other patient and started haemodialysis. I stayed with the young lady all night adjusting medicines and supervising the haemodialysis. I was treating the two patients side by side in the ICU when patient number one woke up and saw me, and we began to talk. Morning came and both patients had survived. Patient number one, Choo Leung, was sure, because I'd stayed with him, that I'd saved his life. He was eternally grateful and, no matter how much I protested over the next several years, he always believed that he was alive because I was right beside him that night.

Mr. Leung eventually went on home haemodialysis, and lived to see the birth of grandchildren and the success of his second restaurant, the Yangtze, in Ottawa's Chinatown.

It has been years since he passed away and I still patronize the Yangtze, which is now the best Chinese restaurant in Ottawa. Today, his son-in-law and grandchildren operate it. They always treat me with the greatest respect.

The other patient, the young lady, recovered her kidney function, returned to Cornwall, and I never heard from her again.

It was an exciting night that ended well but one that definitely had the makings of a double disaster. I don't know how, after working all day, I was able to stay awake and alert all through that long night. I guess it's good to be young – I sure couldn't do it now.

* * *

In the early 1970s, I attended a meeting of the American Society for Artificial Internal Organs in Washington, DC, at which Seattle's Dr. Belding Scribner presented a paper that had a profound effect on me. Dr. Scribner, the leading nephrologist in haemodialysis, told of a haemodialysis patient who became pregnant, carried, and delivered successfully.

It was a very rare occurrence for a patient on dialysis to get pregnant; because of general unwellness, pregnancy and renal failure presented many difficulties to both mother and baby. When pregnancy did occur, the mother was usually advised to have a planned abortion to save her life. However, in this case, the Seattle team had managed the patient's pregnancy and she had delivered a healthy, slightly premature baby. Mother and baby did fine. To me, Dr. Scribner's presentation exemplified the best in nephrology.

In 1986, one of my dialysis patients became pregnant and was determined to have the baby. I pulled no punches with her. I spelled out the myriad problems she could be facing, explained that we would have to follow her extremely carefully, and made her understand that she would require more frequent dialysis.

It seemed to me, in order for her pregnancy to succeed, that we should attempt to keep as low as possible the toxins that are elevated in renal failure. Patients on haemodialysis require a restricted diet because they cannot get rid of toxic products of metabolism through the urine, and require fluid restriction due to their lack of urine output. How were we to allow the fetus to grow and develop normally with restrictions such as those?

We wanted the mother-to-be to have as normal a diet and fluid intake as possible, so we immediately started dialyzing her every day. This regime allowed her to eat normally with no restrictions and to drink as much as necessary whenever she was thirsty.

During her pregnancy many problems presented themselves, such as increased blood pressure and anemia. With a great deal of thought and effort we managed to keep these under control. The baby was growing normally in utero and doing well.

Coincidentally, my wife, Josée, was pregnant at the same time and I was at her bedside while she was in labour. When Josée's doctor, who was also the obstetrician for my pregnant patient, came in, we two medics essentially ignored Josée and wound up talking about our mutual patient, who was six-months pregnant at the time. The obstetrician's nurse gave us both hell and we quickly returned to focusing on my wife. Josée never totally forgave me for that indiscretion, but I'm happy to report that she successfully delivered a healthy baby boy.

As my patient approached thirty-two weeks, we met to decide how we would handle her and the baby. "We" comprised the obstetrician, a pediatric neonatologist, the head nurse of the premature infants' nursery, the head nurse of the case room, the head nurse of the dialysis unit, an anesthesiologist, and me. We had an excellent team, and our meeting was very productive.

The most pressing concern was whether the baby should be delivered vaginally or by caesarian section. After considering all the scenarios, we decided it would be best to deliver her at thirty-four weeks by C-section. The baby was a good size and all signs were good. We decided it would also be best to dialyze the patient before the C-section, rather than after the birth. That way we could let her rest and then do dialysis when she needed it as a normal, non-pregnant patient.

Everything went as planned; the baby weighed five and a half pounds and had an Apgar rating of nine. The Apgar is a rating of how well the baby is at birth – normal is from eight to ten, so nine was wonderful. Both mother and baby, a lovely little girl, did well following delivery. I was very proud of the job done by our team.

I kept a picture of that baby on my office wall and, later, was able to add photos of two additional babies born to dialysis patients whom I looked after.

The Yogi Bear fan club

Back in medical school, three days after writing my pediatrics exam, I received a call instructing me to go to my pediatric professor's office. I couldn't imagine why. While I waited in the anteroom I got all worked up thinking that the only reason a person gets called to a professor's office is if he's in danger of failing – but maybe, just maybe, he'd be given a second chance. I figured I must be in big trouble: in danger of losing my internship at McGill and God knew what else.

I must have waited for a half an hour, totally petrified. When the professor finally called me in, the first thing I asked was if I had failed. "No," he laughed. "You're here to compete for the prize in pediatrics."

It was an oral competition; the professor was conducting one-on-one interviews with the students who had attained the highest grades in the final examination in pediatrics. I was incredibly relieved, but so totally thrown by the experience that I couldn't answer any questions. I wasn't sure that I could get my name right!

I didn't get the prize.

* * *

Between third and fourth year of medical school I spent the summer as an extern at a small hospital. During the month I spent on medicine I worked with an excellent physician who was very knowledgeable and dedicated to his patients. One of his patients was a pleasant man in his sixties whom he was treating for myasthenia gravis, a neuromuscular disorder that leads to muscle weakness and eventual death. At that time, the medication available was short-acting and in time the body became resistant to the drug. The patient lost the power to breathe and thus died. We looked after this gentleman for almost my entire rotation. He was a professor of history and a very interesting person. He and I talked daily and discussed many things from a historical perspective, and I became quite attached to him. Unfortunately, as is common with this disease, he got sicker and had increasing difficulty breathing. He died just before my rotation was finished, and I was very affected by his illness and death.

But the story does not end there.

Many years later, long after I was married, had fathered two sons, and was in practice as a nephrologist in Ottawa, my elder son, Dan, a high school student and aspiring trumpet player, developed a problem: whenever he played his trumpet he lost air through his nose. I took him to see an otolaryngologist (an ear, nose, and throat specialist) who diagnosed myasthenia gravis. My thoughts immediately flew back to my old patient. My then wife Claire, a nurse, was familiar with the condition, too.

We were devastated.

The situation with Dan occurred in 1979 and the treatment, after all these years, was still the short-acting medication that my patient the historian had been given. But the medication treated only the symptoms, not the disease, after which, as with my earlier patient, the sufferer would develop resistance to the medicine, have increasing difficulty breathing, and die.

Being a typical teenager, Dan continued on with his life, playing trumpet in the school band and playing basketball on the school team. He discovered that if he took the pill just before a practice or a game, he was good for three hours. If the practice or the game went longer, he started to weaken and couldn't continue without another pill.

A short while later a new therapy was described that entailed removal of the thymus gland, which is located behind the sternum. Unfortunately, it was not effective in all cases. The procedure required a major operation: opening the chest wall to remove the gland. Following surgery, the patient was usually on a respirator in the intensive care unit for at least a week.

And then a newer technique was developed in New York. In this scenario, the gland was removed with a simple incision in the neck and, post-operative, the patient did not need to be kept in the ICU. We opted for the latter alternative and just as we were arranging the New York procedure, we discovered there was an excellent surgeon doing the same procedure in Toronto. Thankfully, Dan responded well to the operation. Needless to say, we never stopped worrying about him. He returned to basketball and trumpet without any problems and, after graduating from high school, he went on to McGill University to study music.

While he was at McGill, Dan auditioned for a position in the Governor General's Foot Guard, who marched and played daily on Parliament Hill during the summer months. In order to join the band one not only had to be an excellent musician but also had to enlist in the reserve army, which meant having a complete physical examination. Since Dan didn't mention his myasthenia, which had been in remission for five years, and the examining doctor missed the scar on his neck, he was approved for the Canadian Army Reserve. He was sent to an army camp to undergo an intense six-week course of basic training that he got through without incident.

In summertime, the Governor General's Foot Guard marches daily from the governor general's residence on Sussex Drive to Parliament Hill, where it performs the changing of the guard ceremony, then marches back to the barracks. The Guard is always attired in full dress uniform, which includes large bearskin hats. It is mighty warm in that outfit and, on really hot days, it isn't unusual for one or two – or more – of the soldiers to faint.

It was very hot on the day we went to watch Dan's first appearance with the Foot Guard and, of course, we were terribly concerned. We needn't have worried. Dan sailed through without a hitch, continued problem-free all summer long and has been well ever since. Dan now tells me the guys that fainted were all terribly hung over from partying the night before.

My son, Dan, is very fortunate. Today he is a professional trumpet player, is married to a singer/dancer and they have one daughter and a son on the way. He and his wife live in Barcelona, Spain. And now, instead of basketball, he plays and coaches hockey in Barcelona.

I subsequently treated a woman with myasthenia who'd been referred to me because of high blood pressure. We often talked about my son and how well things turned out for him. Unfortunately, the treatment did not work as well for her. She had to take increasing doses of prednisone to control the condition. Prednisone has all sorts of unpleasant side effects, including increasing blood pressure. I continued to see her annually until I retired in 2008.

* * *

After I graduated from the University of Western Ontario Medical School, I went to Montreal to do a year as a rotating intern at the Montreal General Hospital. MGH was part of McGill University, which, at that time, was considered the best medical school in Canada, on par with Johns Hopkins in the United States. Internships at MGH were highly coveted. It was a very exciting time for me.

I drove to Montreal in my awful old Nash Metropolitan – the worst car ever produced – with a classmate, Carolyn Hobbs, who was also interning at MGH. Carolyn was the daughter of Western's assistant dean of medicine and one of only six women in our class. She was a very good student and a great person.

We were feeling very proud of ourselves and very definitely anticipating a warm welcome at our destination. After all, we were real doctors now, not mere medical students, and both of us had graduated with excellent grades.

When we arrived we couldn't find a place to park – which took off a bit of the shine. But, ever aware of our great importance to humanity in general and to McGill in particular, we coped.

MGH sits on the mountain overlooking the city of Montreal. The hospital was relatively new then and Carolyn and I congratulated ourselves on how very nice it was going to be to be housed in this shiny, new facility.

We strode officiously to the front desk of the hospital and announced our arrival. The clerk looked us over and muttered,

"You're just interns. Go to the old building at the end of the hospital." We were taken aback slightly, but we didn't let this put-down faze us.

It took a couple of minutes, but we managed to find the interns' quarters. We'd fully expected to be living in private single rooms in a bright, modern facility. Instead we found ourselves standing in front of an old apartment building that was attached to the beautiful new hospital. The old building had been turned into an interns' residence. But despite this setback we remained positive. We felt certain that very soon someone would realize our importance and accord us the respect we deserved.

We entered the building, marched up to the desk and stated that Drs. Hobbs and Posen were reporting. The receptionist wasn't impressed. She raised an eyebrow and said, "You're interns. You shouldn't be here until tomorrow." That was the last straw. We finally understood that we were on the lowest rung of the ladder.

As it turned out, all forty-eight interns arrived that same day, and utter mayhem ensued. No one had much money and no one had anywhere else to go. Eventually, several rooms with bunk beds were found for the male interns. The women were luckier; the residence had been prepared for the female interns and each one was given her own room.

I got the top bunk in the guys' room. My bunkmate was an Ottawan, Paul Puddicombe, and he and I became good friends. Because both our surnames began with the letter "P," we were put on the same services together for the rest of that internship year. Paul went on to practice obstetrics and gynecology in Ottawa. (Paul's dad, a highly respected OB/GYN in Ottawa, had delivered Princess Juliana of the Netherlands – subsequently Queen Juliana – in the Civic Hospital. The Dutch Royal Family had sought refuge in Ottawa during the Second World War and, in order to have the princess born in her homeland, the hospital room was declared Dutch soil.)

* * *

Every afternoon at 5:30, ten to fifteen MGH interns and residents ran to the interns' lounge. First we'd grab a 25¢ beer from the dispensing machine, then we'd sit ourselves down to watch the Huckleberry Hound Show, starring the greats: Huckleberry Hound, Yogi Bear, and Boo Boo Bear. We called ourselves the Yogi Bear Fan Club.

The group comprised a variety of residents and interns from different services, many of whom went on to become heads of surgery, obstetrics, and various divisions of medicine across Canada. The leader of the pack was the chief resident in medicine, who went on to become a head of medicine and the dean of a Canadian medical school.

This went on all year. If we were in the hospital at 5:30, we'd drop everything – except really sick patients, of course – and head for the TV room.

No one in the club scheduled any activities on weekdays from 5:30 to 6:00 PM. We tried our level best not to miss an episode as long as we were assigned in the main hospital. It was a fantastic stress reliever … and a lot of fun, too!

* * *

In the summer of 1963, after I completed the first year of my residency in medicine at MGH, I took a job as the doctor at Camp Blue Moon in the Laurentian Mountains north of Montreal.

The horseback riding instructor, a woman named Holly, often talked about a friend of hers who was very involved in politics. Not only was he an author and an extreme liberal, he was also leading the revolt against the far-right Union Nationale party, headed by Maurice Duplessis, that was running Quebec at the time. He sounded like a very interesting person.

One Sunday, Holly told me her friend was coming to camp to spend the day with her and she invited me to join them. The three of us had a great time swimming, boating, and talking politics. I was really impressed with him and told her afterwards that I thought he should go into federal politics. "He'd make an excellent prime minister," I said. As it turned out, he did both.

In 1968, when I was practicing nephrology in Ottawa, Pierre Elliott Trudeau, the interesting person with whom I'd spent a delightful summer day years before, was elected prime minister of Canada. Coincidentally, his physician's office was across the hall from mine at the old Ottawa General Hospital and, one day, when the PM came to see his doctor, I went in to say hello. He surprised me by remembering the great day Holly, he, and I had shared. For some reason, my four-year-old son, Dan, was with me, and Trudeau took the time to speak to him and pat him on the head. Forty years later Dan still remembers Trudeau patting him on the head. I'm not sure that the four-year-old Dan understood what it meant to have the prime minister pat him on the head but he bragged about it to his friends then, and treasures the memory to this day.

* * *

During my last year of residency in medicine at the Montreal General Hospital, I decided that I'd like to spend time in the

United States getting additional training in nephrology. So I applied to the Peter Bent Brigham Hospital in Boston, a famous teaching hospital affiliated with Harvard University.

I sent my application to Dr. John Merrill, who was one of the world's foremost nephrologists, and he invited me to interview. I went to Boston, very excited and very nervous. I was an unusual trainee candidate in that I'd had experience with both acute and chronic dialysis and with medical experiments.

Dr. Merrill was late for the appointment. His secretary suggested that I chat with the doctor's assistant until he arrived. The assistant was a renal physiologist who did research on electrolytes in rats, never one of my favorite topics.

He began by quizzing me as if for an examination and we wound up arguing, about what I don't remember. We were actually shouting at each other when Dr. Merrill came in. He sized up the situation and broke us up before we could come to blows. After tempers had cooled, he chuckled and told me that the assistant "often does that for fun."

Meanwhile, I was thinking, "Wow, have I ever screwed up an interview! Here I come, all this way to the Mecca of world medicine, and get into an argument – almost a fist fight – with the great doctor's deputy."

However, despite everything, the interview went very well. Dr. Merrill was very interested in my work with dogs and how increased cerebral spinal fluid pressure caused high blood pressure. We also discussed haemodialysis and its future. We talked for more than two hours. At the end of the interview he asked if I could get Canadian funding for a fellowship because the US wouldn't fund a foreigner. I said I'd look into it and left on a high.

Back in Montreal I discovered that the Canadian Council provided the only funds available to me, and that I was eligible to receive only $3,000 (Canadian) for the year. By then I had a wife and a baby. We couldn't live on that.

I called Dr. Merrill, who said he would try to get me funding, but he wasn't hopeful. A couple of months later he called back. He was very apologetic and regretted to inform me that he couldn't get the funding. I was very disappointed.

Dr. Kaye suggested that I stay with him at MGH for another year, but I wanted to explore other avenues. Another MGH physician, Dr. Francis Chouinard, who was from Baltimore and had contacts there, got me a twelve-month residency in that city. The residency was to be divided; I would do six months as a senior resident in medicine at Baltimore City Hospital, and six months doing nephrology at Johns Hopkins Hospital.

* * *

The first day the chief of nephrology showed me around Johns Hopkins, I knew more people than he did. There were a lot of Canadians there, mainly from McGill.

My six-month stint at Hopkins didn't give me sufficient enough time to sink my teeth into anything really worthwhile, but I made some good friends and valuable contacts. I was impressed at how passionately Hopkins cherished its history and prided itself on the excellence of its patient care, teaching, and research.

While I was in Baltimore, I applied for and got a fellowship in hypertension and nephrology at New York University with two great nephrology hypertensive experts, Dr. Herbert Chasis and Dr. William Goldring. My interview with them went very well and, happily, they had funds under their control. I accepted a two-year program with the understanding that, if all went well, I would go on staff after my two years. Chasis and Goldring were particularly interested in my knowledge of haemodialysis, because they had no one at NYU as knowledgeable in the field.

It was a perfect fit but, unfortunately, it was not to be. The date was 1965 and the US was in the throes of the Vietnam War.

I was thirty when I got the fellowship, too old to be drafted, so I wasn't at all worried about being called up to spend two years in Vietnam. In fact, prior to going to Baltimore, I'd even applied for US immigrant status. That way, in the event that an employment opportunity came up in the US, I could accept it.

We were already apartment hunting seriously in Queens when the US government changed the law, making doctors eligible for the draft until age thirty-five. What this meant was that I had to report to my draft board and would likely be drafted. I had no intention of being drafted. I turned down the position in New York and, at the end of the year, I left Baltimore and returned to McGill. Luckily, Dr. Kaye had a fellowship awaiting me at the Montreal General.

Two years later, when I was working as staff man at the Ottawa General Hospital, I received a letter from the Baltimore draft board instructing me to report for a physical in one week. I knew that if I didn't go I'd be considered a draft dodger and not permitted to enter the US for an undetermined length of time.

I immediately called the US embassy in Ottawa and was eventually put through to someone who said I had to go because I hadn't notified my draft board that I was leaving the country. I said I certainly had done so. "Prove it!" was his reply. I told him the US government knew that I'd left the country because they had my Canadian address. He checked, came back on the line, and agreed that I was not eligible for the draft. In fact, I had even been reclassified as not an immigrant.

After all was said and done, I wound up holding three draft cards: one said I was over age, one said I was eligible for the draft, and one said I was out of the country. Those were the days when people were burning their draft cards; I held onto mine for a long time.

* * *

In 1968 or 1969, three nephrologists, Dr. Art Shimizu, from Hamilton, Dr. Stan Fenton, from Toronto, and I, were doing chronic dialysis in Ontario. We decided it would be advantageous to form our own society in order to lobby the government and make it aware of the needs of patients with chronic renal failure. We formed the Ontario Nephrology Association and quickly attracted membership from all the nephrologists in the province.

In 1970, we realized there was value in being associated with the Ontario Medical Association (OMA). The OMA, which is made up of many sections – surgery, medicine, all the specialties, and family practice – accepted us into their fold.

I served as the first president of the newly formed nephrology section. We wanted to establish more dialysis programs in the province, educate the government and general population, and establish fee schedules.

The executive met monthly in Toronto, usually over lunch on a Friday. This was great for me because my parents lived in Toronto. On those days I'd take an early flight from Ottawa, have breakfast with my mother and lunch at the executive meeting. When the meeting was over, I'd take a streetcar to my father's small hardware store on Queen Street (Regal Hardware still exists and looks the same) in the east end of Toronto, and help out with customers until closing time. Then I'd go home with my father, have a Sabbath meal with my parents, and they'd drive me to the airport to catch my flight back to Ottawa.

I was active on the OMA executive until my parents died, then I decided it was time for newer and younger people to get involved.

* * *

On weekends that I was on call, in addition to seeing to my dialysis patients, I had to make rounds on all the inpatients that were under our care. If the service wasn't too busy I sometimes brought along my son Jacob. He was a welcome diversion for the patients, all of whom enjoyed having a child visit.

One Sunday, when Jacob was about four, a patient with an artificial leg told Jacob that he could do a magic trick. "I can take off my leg," he said, and then he proceeded to do so. Young Jacob was mesmerized. "Daddy," he said, "It must be wonderful to have an artificial leg. I want to be able to take off my leg!"

The patient and I looked at each other for a moment and then laughed long and hard.

* * *

I enjoy teaching, and over the many years since I was an intern I've had the pleasure of teaching many medical classes at the University of Ottawa and at all the Ottawa hospitals.

At one point, I had the responsibility of delivering the Annual Lecture on Potassium Balance in the Body to second-year medical students. Potassium balance is a very complex subject and one which students find very difficult.

I'm usually a reasonably good lecturer, but one year when I was to deliver the lecture I was not at my stellar best. And, in all honesty, the topic is not one of my favorites. That day, the lecture room was full and very warm and, as I droned on, I could see many of the students falling asleep. I have to confess that I was finding my talk so boring that I was on the verge of nodding off myself. Finally, the lecture was over and my captive audience started to leave.

As the last of the students walked out, a six feet four and very muscular student came up to me at the lectern. My initial reaction was that he was going to throw me out the window, which I certainly deserved that day. But, no, it turned out that he had a question.

He introduced himself. His name was Marc Cardinal, and he told me he was a super heavyweight lifter preparing for the 1980 Summer Olympics in Moscow, which were a year and a half away. He said that, in other categories, prior to the weigh-in, contestants made their weight by taking a diuretic. A diuretic is very strong water pill used in heart failure to get rid of excess fluid in the lungs. The athletes did this because the diuretic caused the body to pass additional urine, which led to weight loss. However, a side effect of passing additional urine was the loss of potassium, which caused muscular weakness. In order to counteract the potassium loss the athletes would drink a lot of orange juice, which is very high in potassium, prior to the competition and also ingest potassium in liquid form. The student wanted to know whether the body's potassium could be restored by this method in time for the competition.

It was a good question, but I didn't know the answer and I told him so. I said (in those pre-internet days) that I'd have to look it up in the library, and get back to him. The answer, it turned out, depended on how much time there was between the weigh-in and the actual event. As it turned out, there was enough time to replete the body's potassium.

Marc felt he had a reasonable chance at a winning a bronze medal. In fact, he was so convinced of it that he took his final year off from medical school to train full-time.

Unfortunately, the poor guy never got to compete at the Olympics because, on April 22, 1980, Canada announced it was boycotting the Moscow games to protest Russia's invasion and occupation of Afghanistan. Sixty-four other countries did the same.

The young man was disappointed, of course, but he returned to medical school, graduated, and became a very successful orthopedic surgeon.

* * *

I've often thought how lucky I was to have found medicine and always hoped one of my sons would go into the field. Several years ago, I was teaching a group of third-year medical students when one of them asked if I was Dan Posen's father. I am indeed, and happily admitted it. The young man said he'd known Dan when both of them were studying music at McGill University, but then he decided he couldn't make a living as a musician and went into medicine instead.

He wanted to know all about Dan, of course, so I brought him up to date. I told him Dan was living with a singer/dancer in the old centre of Barcelona, Spain, and playing trumpet for a living. He also had a small jazz band, played sub in the Barcelona Symphony Orchestra, and was doing opera and whatever else he could to scrape by. The medical student confessed he was more than just a little jealous. I, on the other hand, was thinking how much I would have liked Dan to be studying medicine.

Dan married his singer/dancer girlfriend and is still playing trumpet in Barcelona. They have a girl and a son on the way. Now they struggle together, but they love the life.

I am very proud of my sons. All three of them have completed university. The older ones, Dan and Andrew, are doing what they like to do. Andrew is in finance on Wall Street and has four daughters. My youngest, Jacob, has just completed his joint law degree and MBA at Osgoode Hall Law School and the Schulich School of Business, at York University in Toronto.

* * *

Although we had traveled extensively in Canada and overseas, neither Josée nor I had ever visited Newfoundland and Labrador. So, in 1991, we decided to remedy the situation. We planned to fly to St. John's, rent a car, stay at bed and breakfasts, and wander around the province.

A year or so prior to this trip, we'd had a patient from Newfoundland with renal failure in our unit. She'd required a transplant but her sister, the donor, lived in Ottawa and wanted the operation done on her home turf. The nephrology team obliged. I was part of the team that looked after her when I was on call, especially on weekends. (Another colleague, Dr. Shiv Jindal, supervised and followed closely all of our transplant patients). The patient did very well, the transplant worked right away, and there were few, if any, complications.

Being the social animal I am, I got to know the patient and her mother, who accompanied her, very well. They lived on Fogo Island in Newfoundland and Labrador and, when our transplant coordinator learned that my wife and I were traveling to the area, she suggested we might consider going to Fogo Island to drop in and say hello. We thought it a good idea and so, when we were in St. John's we arranged for accommodation at a B & B in the village of Fogo. We didn't tell anyone we were coming.

The patient and her mother lived in the small coastal settlement of Joe Batt's Arm on Fogo Island just a short distance from our B & B. The landlady knew the family and gave us directions to the community. When we arrived we had no trouble getting directions to their house; in that small a settlement everyone not only knew the house but knew we'd find mother and daughter at home.

Mother answered our knock and was speechless when she saw us. She was so excited to see me that she burst into tears of joy and enveloped me in a big bear hug. Then she called Daughter who took one look at me, burst into tears and wrapped her arms around me in a massive hug exactly like mom's.

Mother insisted we stay for supper and sent her daughter down to the pier to get a fresh cod. The fish she brought back was huge, maybe two feet in length.

I watched as Mother prepared the fish for cooking. First she poured salt on the open fish and I remarked, "that seems like a lot of salt." (We nephrologists are anti-salt, as it can lead to high blood pressure if used to excess). Mother laughed and said she was "going easy" because she knew her daughter was on a low-salt diet! The fish was baked and served. Never before or since have I ever eaten better tasting fish.

Some of their relatives joined us at supper and one of the cousins asked if Josée and I would like to go jigging for cod in the morning. We said yes … and then we found out what jigging for cod entailed! I'm not so sure, if we'd known before, that we would have agreed so readily. Nevertheless, we'd committed to go and go we would. We were instructed to eat some breakfast at our B & B, then meet back at the house at 5:00 AM. From there we'd go out in an open dinghy with a small motor.

When we awoke the next morning it was still black outside. We dressed, quickly ate the breakfast our landlady had left for us, and drove back to the house where we found … another larger breakfast waiting for us!

After the second breakfast, we walked to the dock, changed into rubber suits, and off we went. My poor wife! At the best of times she doesn't like the water – and here we were, wet and cold, in a small dinghy on the North Atlantic. The cousin taught us how to jig our hooks and jig the lines up and down. Although our teacher had a small sonar machine that helped to locate the fish, we caught absolutely nothing – that was the time when people were beginning to realize the fish were disappearing – but it was a wonderful experience.

At 10:00 AM, we beached on a small island called Little Fogo where we tucked into a wonderful lunch that Mother had sent. At one time there had been a settlement on Little Fogo, but it had closed down because the kids who lived there couldn't get to school. After lunch we walked around the island and ate wild berries, before heading back home – where Mother had prepared another enormous lunch for us. It was about 11:30 AM and already we'd had two breakfasts and two lunches! Our second lunch was as excellent as the first. Now, stuffed to the gills, we headed back to the B & B to rest, but not before promising to return for a barbecue that evening, because more cousins and relatives wanted to meet us. From our room at the B & B we watched a giant iceberg float by and then we fell into a deep sleep.

The barbecue was wonderful – all the steak you can imagine, and then some. We were treated like royalty. It was very touching, and especially gratifying because we could see how well the patient had done. After supper we all sat around and there was singing and storytelling. The next day we left, taking with us the memory of an unforgettable and very special experience.

* * *

After I retired at age seventy-five and gave up my medical and dialysis clinics, I decided to volunteer at the Civic campus of The Ottawa Hospital. The commitment involves one half-day a week working at the main information desk answering questions and directing patients and visitors. Fortunately, I usually work with an experienced and delightful woman, Hazel Warren, who's been at it a lot longer than I have and knows a whole lot more than I do.

One day a very attractive woman came up to the desk. She looked to be in her early forties and seemed familiar, but I couldn't immediately place her. She certainly knew me because she addressed me by name and proceeded to tell me she was well, asked how I was enjoying retirement, and added that, although the nephrologist and liver specialist looking after her now were very good, she missed me. We chatted about generalities until I got busy and she left. After she walked away I remembered who she was.

I first saw her perhaps fifteen years ago when she was referred because of polycystic kidney disease. This is a relatively common hereditary disease that leads to kidney failure. Patients with polycystic kidney disease develop cysts in the kidneys that enlarge and encroach on normal tissue until kidney function gradually deteriorates over time. The patient often develops high blood pressure early on so it is important to delay the onset of renal failure with good blood pressure control and medicine that strengthens the body and bones.

Another problem that occurs, more frequently in women than in men, is the development of additional cysts in the liver. The cysts don't affect liver function but may cause it to become enormous, which was what had happened to this patient. When she was referred to me her abdomen was getting so large she had trouble eating and she looked ten-months pregnant. In addition, her energy level was falling – the large mass in her abdomen made it difficult for her to eat and her arms and legs were thin. She looked anorexic. I was very concerned.

There had been occasional reports of this type of liver being removed and followed by a successful liver transplant. In Canada, the procedure was being done only in London, Ontario, so I referred her there. Initially, the physicians in London didn't want to accept her as a candidate because, although her liver had become enormous, her liver function was normal. However, I persisted, and they finally agreed to put her on the transplant list. It had taken some time but about three years after I started working with her she'd had the enormous liver removed and a new liver transplanted. Her kidney function stabilized and she did well.

I had seen her a few times post-transplant and she kept improving. She ultimately was eating normally and was able to return to her high-pressure government job. She looked so good the day she stopped by the information desk that I didn't recognize her. It was very gratifying to see her so well and so normal.

Murder by methanol

It was Christmas Eve and we were having a festive dinner at my cousin's home. We'd just sat down to eat when I received a call from a doctor in Hull, Quebec, just across the river from Ottawa. He had a patient who was quite ill and not passing any urine. What did I think was wrong and would I accept transfer? I agreed to the transfer but as for what was wrong, I said I'd have to see the patient before I could make a diagnosis.

I informed the Civic emergency that a patient was being transferred, instructed them to call me when he arrived, and alerted the ICU that he would probably require admission there. Needless to say, he arrived at the Civic before the main course was served, and I left to the hospital directly and met the man in an emergency room.

It was obvious that he was severely ill and exhibiting other signs that suggested methanol intoxication. Methanol (wood alcohol) poisoning is very rapidly lethal, leading first to blindness, then to death. Methanol can be removed from the body quickly by haemodialysis, so I set in motion the order to start it. At the same time, to be certain of the diagnosis, I ordered his blood taken for toxicology testing.

We called in an on-call nurse who, although she was a nurse manager, had no experience with acute dialysis. So we called in a second, very experienced nephrology nurse. The two nurses rushed to the nephrology unit to prepare the dialysis machine. I also called in my resident who was invaluable in carrying out treatment according to my orders.

I was so sure methanol was the culprit that I decided to start therapy immediately. The therapy consists of intravenous alcohol, which prevents the breakdown of methanol into its more toxic particles (methanoic, or formic, acid). These toxic particles are what cause the severe acidosis that leads to renal failure and death. In cases involving methanol, even if the patient survives, the toxic particles may cause blindness – hence the necessity of the alcohol to bind the toxins until they can be removed by haemodialysis.

The big question was where the methanol had come from. No one in the patient's family could make a connection with anything vaguely akin to methanol. And then someone said that two nights earlier the whole family had attended an engagement party where homemade punch was served. It became immediately clear that that could be the cause of the problem.

I instructed my medical student and the Hull police to contact every single person who had attended the party and tell them to come to emergency at the Civic Hospital, and fast. I arranged with the emergency staff to triage all the individuals as they arrived. In all, thirty-six people showed up. Each was questioned about their vision and had their blood tested for methanol. Anyone who was sick or experiencing vision problems was sent directly to the dialysis unit to receive an IV with alcohol and prepare for haemodialysis. In fact, the alcohol infusions were started in the emergency even before the patients were sent to dialysis.

In addition to the patient who was already being dialyzed, we had to dialyze three others and keep a few whose levels were not in the toxic range under observation in emergency. In all, four people required haemodialysis.

When the referred patient arrived at the hospital he'd been in a deep coma. His methanol levels were very high and he required a respirator because he was unable to breathe on his own. We dialyzed him until the methanol was removed from his system and his electrolytes were normal. Even so, we feared he was brain-dead: though he was still on the respirator, he was totally unresponsive. When dialysis was completed we transferred him to the ICU where they followed him for a few more hours. Eventually he was evaluated by neurology and our diagnosis was confirmed. At that point the coroner was called in because now the situation had become a criminal case.

A warrant was issued for the person who'd made the punch, but the police soon discovered that he'd fled the country. Off to Lebanon, and there was no treaty to bring him back.

Meanwhile, the other three patients, two of whom were admitted with vision difficulties, got better with dialysis and their vision returned to normal. The third patient was asymptomatic but we dialyzed her anyway because she had high levels of methanol. They all came off dialysis in the morning and were discharged.

When I conducted a further investigation, talking to the people who had been at the party, I learned that the deceased had drunk the methanol-laced punch but no other alcohol. That was what did him in. Because alcohol counteracts the effects of methanol, those who drank both punch and alcohol were protected from methanol poisoning by the alcohol. One asymptomatic woman who registered high levels of methanol admitted to drinking at least a whole bottle of wine. The bottle of wine was what saved her.

(As it happens, the three party guests who required dialysis and received a simultaneous infusion of alcohol became quite drunk, and soon after began to sing racy songs in Arabic. We knew they were racy because my resident, who was from Kuwait, translated them for us.)

* * *

Meanwhile, my wife, Josée, had remained at my cousin's for dinner, returned home alone, and went to bed. Like most doctors' wives, she was used to my working late and being called in early and so, when the phone rang at 6:15 AM, she assumed I would answer it. When the ringing persisted she realized I wasn't there and rolled over to pick up the phone. The person on the line spoke with a strong Quebecois accent and identified himself as Sgt. Charbonneau of the Hull police force. Josée immediately had visions that I was in some dreadful difficulty across the river or had been in an accident. The sergeant assured her that I was fine, in no trouble with the law, and apologized for disturbing her at this ungodly hour. He explained that he'd missed me at the hospital, knew I was en route home, and asked that she have me call him when I arrived.

What the sergeant wanted was my statement regarding the events, which I duly gave him. But since the man who made the punch had escaped to Lebanon, the case was put on hold – though not forgotten.

Incredibly, twelve years later, I got a call from the same sergeant to tell me that the suspect had been picked up at the border attempting to enter Canada. Now that the man was in custody there would be a preliminary hearing which I was expected to attend. The sergeant explained that, after the hearing, a decision would be made as to whether the accused would be tried for manslaughter or murder. Fortunately, I had kept voluminous notes throughout the treatments and the discharges because I realized very early on that this case probably had legal overtones.

At the hearing, the defence tried to prove that the deceased patient had not been murdered by the accused because it had been the hospital staff who had shut off the respirator – thereby causing the patient's demise! Although no decision was made as to whether the charge would be murder or manslaughter, it was determined the case would go to trial.

I heard nothing for several months and eventually called the officer for an update. And what an update! He told me there would be no trial because all the material for the case had been lost in a move to new police headquarters!

And so it ended.

If nothing else, the situation had been excellent practice for a disaster. Everyone involved had reacted swiftly and professionally. The head nurse who had never seen an acute dialysis patient did a great job helping the veteran nurse. The emergency room staff, the physicians, nurses, lab technicians, and porters all did their jobs superbly. Getting people to the ER, getting them examined, their blood taken, transported, and analyzed – everything went unbelievably smoothly. My resident was at my side all night and a medical student did triage in the emergency with the emergency doctors. I couldn't have done it without them. I was tremendously proud of how the hospital team came together and accomplished this Herculean task.

The referred patient was probably brain-dead by the time he arrived at the hospital, but the others all returned to normal, lost no vision, and were well.

* * *

About two years after the disastrous engagement party, I received a call from a doctor at National Defence Medical Centre (NDMC) concerned about possible methanol poisoning among several soldiers stationed at Canadian Forces Base Petawawa, about one hundred and fifty kilometres northwest of Ottawa.

Apparently, one hundred soldiers had attended a party off the base and now one of them was quite sick and exhibiting symptoms that sounded very much like methanol poisoning.

From 1967 to 1985, I was the nephrologist responsible for the NDMC, which was equipped to handle patients but did not have a dialysis unit. I immediately arranged with the NDMC physician to transport those who were sick or experiencing vision problems to the Civic Hospital for dialysis. When the remaining ninety or so soldiers triaged at NDMC were examined, had blood gasses taken for acidosis and methanol levels drawn, it was determined that four required dialysis for vision or acidosis.

The first soldier sent to us died en route to the hospital. But, fortunately, with dialysis, the other three made full recoveries. The situation of the first soldier was similar to that of the patient who died after the engagement party. Like him, the soldier hadn't drunk any other alcohol, he'd drunk only the punch which contained the methanol. Without alcohol in his system to protect him from the effects of methanol he became extremely sick and succumbed to the methanol poisoning. The soldiers who required dialyzing had drunk an amount of alcohol but not enough to combat the methanol.

The moral of the story is: if you're going to drink a poison such as methanol, you're better off getting roaring drunk with other booze at the same time.

* * *

Long before these methanol encounters, as a first year resident at the Montreal General, I was among several residents who were sent to Charlotte, North Carolina, as part of a rotation.

In Charlotte, we not only acted as residents who looked after a ward with staff men, we were also responsible for medical consults to the emergency room. Whenever a patient had to be seen or to be admitted to the ER, they called one of us. I was on call every other day.

I once had as a patient a woman who came in from the hills of North Carolina. Her case was really confusing. She was in severe renal failure and severely anemic. She had all sorts of pains and problems, very low blood pressure, and low urine output.

I worked very hard on her. I read everything I could lay my hands on to figure out what ailed her but I just couldn't make a real definitive diagnosis. I kept asking her if she'd had an infection recently, or eaten or drunk anything unusual. It sounded like we were dealing with a toxin but we couldn't figure out what and where it could have come from. I was really at a loss as to what to do.

I treated her symptomatically but felt very bad because I was quite sure she was going to die and I still couldn't determine the cause of her illness. My staff man was equally confused. Although I was treating her, I didn't know if I was treating her with the right things.

Then, to my great surprise, and that of everyone else, the lady started to get better and, after two or three weeks in hospital, she was discharged. As she was leaving, she said, "Thank you very much, Dr. Posen. You were a great help to me and I appreciate what you have done."

It was then that she told me that prior to being admitted to hospital she had been drinking White Lightning.

"Pardon?" I said.

She repeated, "White Lightning."

I had no idea what White Lightning was, but my colleagues and staff men did: White Lightning is moonshine made in the North Carolina hills, often in old battery cases. When my colleagues heard she'd been ingesting White Lightning they knew that she had lead, arsenic, and various other poisons in her.

The lady knew exactly what was causing her distress but didn't want to get anybody into trouble. She was willing to die rather than to tell me about it.

* * *

Many years later, as I was making rounds at the Ottawa General one weekend, an elderly woman in her eighties complained of dizziness. She felt as if the room was spinning, had a strange sensation of not feeling right, and kept bursting into unprovoked laughter. I examined her and could find nothing specific but, when I went over her medication, I noted that she was getting one ounce of brandy every four hours. I had written this as, "Brandy: one ounce as required at bedtime only when necessary (qhs prn)." However, it had been mistakenly transcribed as to give her one ounce every four hours (whether she needed it or not). The poor woman, a total abstinent, was drunk and didn't know it.

The story has a happy ending: stopping the brandy worked and I never again ordered it for her.

In those days brandy was an acceptable bedtime sedative; now it is not. I often wonder if it was my terrible handwriting that confused the nurses. Fortunately, today, pharmaceutical orders are checked and rechecked by the pharmacists and, since most hospitals are using computer order entry, there is no bad handwriting to misinterpret.

* * *

As an intern, I once admitted a young man of my age – twenty-five – for acute alcoholism and heart failure. He had a congenital heart defect that was non-operable but his heart condition could be relatively well controlled. However, his drinking, coupled with the heart disease, was going to kill him.

At the time, there was a popular folk song called "Tom Dooley," the first verse of which was:

> *Hang down your head, Tom Dooley,*
> *Hang down your head and cry;*
> *Hang down your head, Tom Dooley,*
> *Poor boy, you're bound to die.*

Coincidentally, this patient's name was *Don* Dooley. I spent as much time with him as I could and I'd often sing, "Hang down your head, *Don Dooley*, poor boy you're bound to die." I have a terrible voice, and my attempts at singing would make both of us laugh like crazy.

I spent many, many hours trying to convince the fellow that he had to give up drinking. I suggested that he join AA, and he promised he'd follow it up. Unfortunately, about a month after he was discharged he was readmitted with severe alcohol intoxication and heart failure, and he died. Despite all my attempts to get through to him, he had not gone to AA, he'd just started drinking again. His death struck me hard, and since then I have tried not to get emotionally involved with patients.

North by northwest

I'd always had a yearning to go to Africa or some other developing area of the world, and while I was interning at the Montreal General I began making arrangements to do so as soon as my internship was over.

Before I could solidify my plans, Dr. Cameron, chief of medicine at McGill, called me into his office and suggested strongly that I'd be of much greater use to developing countries if I finished my training in internal medicine before going. He was very persuasive and convinced me to stay in the program rather than go to a far-flung subcontinent. However, by the time I finished my training, I was married and the father of two young children. At that point, going off to Africa to work in the jungle for a year or more was no longer an option. But I never lost the desire to travel.

In 1969, I was working as a nephrologist in charge of the dialysis unit at the Ottawa General Hospital. I had just bought a new station wagon and didn't have extra money for a vacation, so I decided it would be interesting to take a locum in the far north. The remuneration was very good and would cover the expense of taking my family with me.

I was fortunate to get a locum doing general practice in the Northwest Territories. I would be spending two weeks in Fort Smith, along the border with Alberta, and three weeks in Yellowknife, the territorial capital. I would be the only physician in both places. During the summer no other doctors were available in small northern towns.

* * *

One day, a dirty, scraggy individual of indeterminate age showed up in the Yellowknife office. He looked, and was, terribly sick. He had a temperature of 104 degrees, severe shaking chills, and knees and elbows that were swollen and hot. Green pus was pouring out of his penis.

I diagnosed gonococcus septicemia with arthritis and told the poor fellow that he had a good chance of recovering but I'd have to admit him to hospital and start him on therapy. Having trained at the shrine of Canadian medicine, McGill University, where I had seen many difficult cases, I knew that treating the condition required high intravenous doses of the latest and best antibiotics. Without this treatment, he had no chance.

Or so I thought.

As I was arranging for the fellow to be admitted and to get started on treatment, he spoke up.

"Sorry, Doc," he said. "There's no way I'm going into hospital."

I was flabbergasted. I tried to reason with him, explaining yet again the severity of his illness and how, very likely, he'd die within the next day or two if he didn't get the full complement of intravenous antibiotics.

"Sorry, Doc," he said again. "You'll have to do something else. I'm not going into hospital."

I asked if he was afraid of hospitals. That wasn't it. He explained that he was a prospector, and a group of rich Americans was on its way up to look at his stake.

"If they buy it," he said, "I'll be a multimillionaire."

I told him he was going to be a dead multimillionaire. He said it didn't matter – he would take the gamble. So I gave him the highest dose of antibiotics that I could give him intramuscularly into his buttocks. The poor man had a very sore bum by the time I finished. I also gave him some oral antibiotics and off he went. I was quite sure he would be dead within a day or two at the most.

About a week later I was walking along the street when a guy in his thirties came up and threw his arms around me. I had no idea who he was.

"Hey, Doc," he said, "thank you very much. You saved my life!"

I looked at him. "Pardon me?"

"Don't you remember me, Doc?" he said. "I had high fever and awful pain in my knees and elbows."

I was blown away. "My God, you're all right!" And then: "How were the Americans? Are you a multimillionaire?"

He shrugged his shoulders and said, "Nope. It didn't pan out. There was no gold there."

I used to tell this story to my medical students and then ask what they'd have done if they were in this situation. Would they have gone into hospital or gambled it all and gone into the bush?

* * *

In addition to attending to the medical requirements of Fort Smith and Yellowknife, I was also responsible for the health of people living in isolated First Nations settlements. This involved both phone consults as well as flying into some settlements every week.

I was flown into settlements in a four-seater Cessna floatplane. We'd land in the nearest body of water and taxi to the dock, where I'd be picked up by someone from the settlement and driven to the nurses' station to start the clinic. I saw patients all day long, slept in the nurses' station overnight, and was picked up the next day for the flight back.

One locale was so windy that the plane couldn't get in to the dock when it returned to pick me up. The pilot, who was standing atop of the float and using a paddle to keep the plane from getting away on the lake, told me to take my medical and overnight bags and wade back to shore. I thought it would make a great picture. So when I got to shore I gave my camera to one of the nurses, and then waded part way back out with all my paraphernalia. I still have the picture – and it is pretty great. The pilot, however, was not amused. He couldn't believe that I was horsing around while he was straining to keep the plane from escaping. He threatened to leave me behind, but of course he didn't. By the time we arrived back in Yellowknife we were friends and laughing about it.

The next week, the same pilot flew me to Fort Chipewyan, a First Nations settlement on Lake Athabasca in the far north of Alberta. As we flew over Wood Buffalo National Park, we were treated to the sight of huge herds of buffalo. The pilot started to teach me to fly on that trip, letting me handle the controls all the way to the Fort. Forty years later I took real flying lessons.

Fort Chipewyan was situated in a very beautiful area. At that time it was a wonderful place to live and boasted excellent game and plenty of fish. Unfortunately, the oil sands runoff has contaminated the lake, and now there is a lot of illness in the community that didn't exist forty years ago.

Each settlement had a small nurses' station and two resident nurses who saw to the settlement's basic medical needs. The visiting doctor would run a clinic to deal with the serious problems the nurses had documented since his last visit and follow chronic patients such as diabetics and those with high blood pressure. The nurses were very competent and very devoted to their job. When a problem arose they would call me and together we'd decide whether to treat it there or fly the patient to Yellowknife or Edmonton.

One nurse had a pet dog that was part retriever. The only things available to throw were rocks, so she and I would throw them for the dog to fetch. That dog would bring back the rock as gently as if she was carrying a duck in her mouth.

Northern nursing came with its own set of risks, not the least of which was that a nurse had to accompany any patient who had to be flown out for treatment. A few months after my visit, the nurse who owned the dog tragically died in a plane that crashed during a storm. She was flying out with a woman who had gone into premature labour.

In the lab

In 1963–64, the Montreal General was just beginning a chronic haemodialysis program. We were dialyzing with a coil dialyzer (a type of artificial kidney that was very efficient) and using a common bath for the dialysate.

A new patient, a man in his forties, had started dialysis. But each time as the dialysis progressed, he would develop a severe headache and his blood pressure would spike. We had no idea what was causing the problem or how to treat it. We used every blood pressure medication available to try to lower his blood pressure but we were unsuccessful. The only thing that helped was stopping the dialysis treatment.

I felt his problem may have been caused by cerebral edema (swelling of the brain) brought about by the too rapid removal of toxins – mainly urea – from the blood. Since toxins remain in the brain before diffusing into the blood stream, they could cause fluid to be drawn into the brain and cause it to swell. This could explain the headache.

That swelling of the brain can cause high blood pressure is a fact that was first demonstrated in the late nineteenth century by Harvey Cushing, a physician and neurosurgeon at Johns Hopkins University. Dr. Cushing showed in animals and humans that as the pressure in the brain increased, the body reacted by trying to maintain blood flow to the brain by increasing the blood pressure. I thought this was happening in my patient and believed, if we could reproduce it in animals, that maybe we could discover a way to treat or prevent it. Dr. Kaye, the chief of nephrology, liked my idea – and he had some discretionary funds at his disposal.

It was quite a job to set up, but I received a lot of help from the animal technicians. I employed Dr. Cushing's methods for measurement, using dogs that were in renal failure. The idea was simple: make the dogs uremic (that is, induce renal failure) by tying off their ureters (the tubes leading from the kidneys to the bladder), wait a few days, anesthetize them, put them on the artificial kidney, and measure their blood and brain pressure. The results were exactly as Dr. Cushing had described: as the pressure in the brain increased, the body reacted by trying to maintain blood flow to the brain by increasing the blood pressure.

In one of the experiments absolutely nothing happened and when we studied the blood result we discovered the dog wasn't in renal failure. Afterwards, when I did an autopsy on the dog, I found that I had tied off the fallopian tubes instead of the ureters. In other words, I didn't create renal failure, I created birth control. I knew then that I wasn't cut out to be a surgeon.

Once the results were in we tried different methods to treat the brain swelling on my patient. They were successful. He no longer had headaches or severe high blood pressure and we realized the way to avoid the problems was to give him slower and more frequent dialysis, as well as a better diet with less protein. Unfortunately for us, Dr. John Dossetor and a group at the Royal Victoria in Montreal were doing the same experiment and published their results before we finished, so I never published ours. Nonetheless, the experiment was very helpful in learning about and preventing a dreadful complication in haemodialysis. In particular, we solved the problem in our patient and he stayed on dialysis for at least ten years, no longer plagued by problems of headache and high blood pressure.

It always fascinates me how much we can learn from those who went before. Imagine: I was repeating an experiment that was done in the 1890s! What a brilliant man Dr. Cushing was – so very ahead of his time.

* * *

During 1967, one of my projects was to study hypoparathyroidism in the rat. The parathyroid glands are four small glands that lie under the thyroid in the neck. These glands put out a parathyroid hormone that is very important in regulating calcium absorption and bone metabolism. In other words, very important for strong bones.

In order to make the rat hypoparathyroidic, we had to anesthetize the rodent to remove the four small parathyroid glands in the neck. The parathyroid glands are very small in both rats and humans and, since our lab didn't have a dissecting microscope that would have magnified the area, the procedure was very difficult. Two days later we were to measure the serum calcium. If the procedure was successful, the serum calcium would be low and we could try different medications to raise calcium levels. Unfortunately, I didn't succeed in removing the parathyroid glands from even one of the hundred rats I dealt with, so the experiment went no further.

I learned two lessons from this. First, without question, I was not cut out to be a surgeon (a truth I knew from my previous experiments with dogs). And, second, I understood that I didn't have the stomach or patience to do lab research.

The dog that couldn't pee

In the early 1970s, I was working with a scientist veterinarian from the National Research Council, researching kidney transplants in dogs. It is fairly easy to transplant kidneys between dogs because the surgery is not difficult, and you don't have to match them. They were very useful for studies on transplantation.

Eventually, the NRC colleague with whom I was working decided to go into private practice in the east end of Ottawa. One evening in 1971, a week or two before Christmas, he called me with a problem: a family had brought in a dog that was very ill. The animal was in kidney failure and close to death. Would I consider doing a transplant on the dog with him? I agreed to look at the animal and see if we could do something besides a transplant.

My examination determined that the animal had acute pyelonephritis (a kidney infection) and was, indeed, in acute renal failure. Immediate dialysis was necessary to save his life. We started treatment with intravenous antibiotics and peritoneal dialysis, replacing fluid in the abdomen every so often.

The dog was dialyzed at the vet's clinic and after three or four days the kidneys got better and the dog was his usual frisky self. The pooch was discharged in good condition two days before Christmas.

That was the first and only time I ever did peritoneal dialysis on a dog. During my residency I had experimented with haemodialysis on dogs, but never peritoneal.

But there is more to this story.

As I was making rounds in the Civic Hospital dialysis unit one evening in 1998, I saw a patient who I had started on peritoneal dialysis about two years previously. He was doing well initially but developed one of the complications – severe infection of the peritoneum. He then had to be changed to chronic haemodialysis. The man gazed at me for a long minute, then said, "You won't remember me, but I had a dog…"

As soon as I heard him utter those words I knew it was the dog from twenty-seven years earlier, in 1971. The patient told me how important it had been to his children that their dog had come home before Christmas. "My family always speaks of that Christmas as the best Christmas ever," he said.

The intriguing thing, of course, was that after treating the dog for peritoneal dialysis, twenty-five years later I had treated its owner for the same condition.

At one point during his treatment, this patient was in serious difficulty because we ran out of blood vessels to attach him to the dialysis machine for haemodialysis. Another doctor told him it was the end of the road, and advised him to get his affairs in order and prepare for death. Needless to say, he was devastated.

By happy circumstance, I had just returned from a special meeting in Colorado that focused on access for haemodialysis. A paper was presented regarding a new technique for patients in a similar situation to this man. Although the technique had been used only a few times, it made eminent sense to try it. I discussed it with the patient and with my radiology colleagues, and everyone – patient and radiologists – immediately agreed.

Miraculously, it worked! Subsequently we used it in other patients in similar dire states.

The man with the dog worked as a tombstone engraver and, years later, when I had my first operation for lung cancer, he carved the word DESIRE on a small rock and gave it to me. I think by *desire* he meant *will to live*. That stone still sits on the hutch over my desk at home. That patient went on to live for many years. He eventually died of a heart attack.

The story does not end there. This year, 2014, while playing bridge at a club, one of my opponents ask if I was Dr. Posen. She then told me her husband was my patient with the dog and thanked me for everything.

* * *

When I was a senior resident in medicine in Montreal, I was assigned to the Queen Mary Veterans' Hospital for two months and put in charge of two junior residents. Both Henry Haddad and Doug Pollick were excellent doctors and we worked together very well. It was the most exciting, stimulating period in my training, because we were one of two teams competing for excellence across several areas. The other team was from the Royal Victoria Hospital.

Each team was responsible for a ward of thirty patients. The teams would see patients in emergency (alternating on call every other day) and admit them to their assigned ward. My two junior residents and I, under the supervision of two staff men from the Montreal General, were responsible for the total care of the thirty patients on our ward. The Royal Victoria team was set up exactly the same way: senior resident, two juniors, and staff men from the Royal Vic.

The cases were presented at weekly conferences that included the residents, staff men, and nurses. The teams competed on how well their patients did; the complexity of the cases; presentations; research; how much more one team knew than the other; and on how quickly a team's patients got better and out of hospital.

There was always, until the hospitals merged, great competition between the MGH and the Vic. In this situation, each institution was out to prove that it was the better hospital and had the better doctors. Thus, the whole team pulled together, worked very hard, and was fastidious in looking after patients.

One day on our ER rotation we got a call to the emergency – *stat* – where an old alcoholic man had presented with a cough, blood in his sputum, and severe shortness of breath. My junior resident Doug Pollick and I arrived at the same time; Henry stayed behind to handle the ward. Doug began an examination of the patient, who was drunk and combative. Undeterred, Doug, who was a large, strong man, insisted as usual on doing a complete examination.

We were masked because of the danger of tuberculosis in this type of alcoholic individual and, as Doug was doing the exam, the patient tore off Doug's facemask. I asked Doug to stop the examination and get a new mask, but he continued.

The patient continued to cough, now right in Doug's face. After we got him settled and took an X-ray of his chest, we discovered the patient had active tuberculosis. Doug subsequently developed TB and had to be treated for six months. He recovered, finished his training, and became an internist on Vancouver Island. Henry became head of gastroenterology at Sherbrooke University in Quebec.

* * *

In 1964, the transplant of human kidneys had begun in a few centres, including the Royal Victoria Hospital in Montreal under the leadership of Dr. John Dossetor. Dr. Kaye of MGH felt that we should also get into it. We had a patient, a forty-year-old man, who was not doing well on dialysis and his wife wanted to donate a kidney to him. That was in the early days, when there was no such thing as crossmatch testing to check to see if the kidneys were compatible. The surgeon was convinced it was not a difficult operation and he practiced the procedure on dogs. I was in the operating room to observe the real operation. The surgery went well but as soon as the blood flowed into the new kidney it went purple. It never functioned. The patient had a stormy post-operative course and died. Later, we realized that there was an incompatibly between the wife's and husband's tissues. The tests we do now would have shown that, but they were not available at that time. This event stopped transplantation at the Montreal General for many years. It remained for the Royal Victoria and Dr. Dossetor to do renal transplants. This separation helped the Royal Victoria develop a first rate program.

* * *

In 1969, very few kidney transplants were performed in Ottawa. Donors and patients had to be related, and very few patients had parents or siblings available to donate a kidney. In 1968, the diagnosis of brain death as a criterion for transplantation from non-family donors was beginning to be used – initially in the US, then spreading across the world. New laws were passed that supported the diagnosis.

The diagnosis of brain death needs to be rigorous, in order to be certain that the condition is irreversible. Legal criteria vary, but in general they require neurological examinations by two independent physicians. The exams must show complete and irreversible absence of brain function, which means that the patient has no brain activity but is kept alive by a respirator and the heart. It also requires that the patient show no electrical activity in the brain (a flat electroencephalogram), no reflexes, not be on any drugs, be assessed by two separate physicians twenty-four hours apart, and neither physician have any contact or relation to the kidney team. If all these conditions are met, the kidney team can then shut off the respirator and observe for five minutes any sign of attempted breathing or reflexes. If nothing occurs, the patient is officially pronounced dead. Life support, in the form of the respirator, is restarted until the organs – the kidneys, and other organs such as the heart, liver, and lungs – are removed to be transplanted into other patients.

I presented this to the medical board and the executive of the hospital. It took some convincing but eventually they agreed to try it. In those days without helmets, motorcyclists were frequently head injured and brain-dead after an accident. We of course had to explain the situation to the relatives and get permission to use the organs. At that time, no one knew anything about this kind of transplantation.

The surgeons were hesitant at first about doing a transplant of this kind, but I convinced them and we went ahead. We used one of the kidneys at the Ottawa General, and the other I took in a police car, sirens wailing and the major roads shut down, across town to the Civic, where a patient was waiting. That was the first time kidneys were shared across town, and this led to a news release and a large news conference in the board room of the hospital. We were interviewed by the CBC and CTV television networks and many newspapers. The operations went well and thus began the major combined transplant program in Ottawa.

Something in the water

Although severe bone problems were common in chronic haemodialysis patients, none of our patients at the MGH had a problem with bone disease, nor with the equally common condition neuropathy (loss of feeling in the periphery of the legs and feet, and weakness going on to paralysis of the foot and ankle). Dr. Kaye, the chief of nephrology, speculated that we were doing something that was preventing our dialysis patients from experiencing these problems, and directed me to research why this was happening. I was to learn a new technique for measuring serum magnesium – an element that is found normally in the blood – measure it in our patients, and compare the results to normal people, whose levels of magnesium were already well established.

We were using plain tap water in the electrolyte bath and speculated that magnesium might be high in the water. Since we were adding magnesium in the electrolyte bath perhaps it was leading to high magnesium in the blood, thus preventing bone disease and neuropathy.

I measured the serum levels of magnesium before and after dialysis and confirmed that our patients had a higher level of magnesium than normal. Next, I studied the Montreal water and found it contained significant magnesium, which would explain why the magnesium went up in dialysis treatment. I read all available medical literature on magnesium but found no evidence to support our theory. However, in the absence of anything else, we proposed that our high levels of magnesium after dialysis were what prevented bone disease and neuropathy in our patients.

At the end of my fellowship year, in June, 1967, I attended the European Dialysis and Transplant Society Meeting in Paris, France, where I presented our data and conclusions that high magnesium helped prevent bone and neurological disease.
Immediately following my presentation a group from Glasgow, Scotland, presented data that had led them to conclude just the opposite. It turned out that we were both wrong. Many factors contributed to our success – mainly long dialysis and lack of aluminum and/or fluoride in the Montreal water – but magnesium was not one of them. Dr. Adam Linton, the nephrologist who presented the paper from Scotland, ultimately moved to Canada and became head of nephrology at the Victoria Hospital at the University of Western Ontario. We became good friends and had many a chuckle about our opposite conclusions.

* * *

In Montreal, Dr. Kaye was always very interested in bone disease in general and bone disease in dialysis patients in particular. Indeed, none of our dialysis patients at MGH developed severe bone disease.

And then I came to Ottawa.

In Ottawa, I discovered that our patients at the General Hospital had terrible bone pains. They'd cough and fracture their ribs, fall, or bump into things and fracture whatever bone was involved.

I was thirty-three, thought I knew everything there was to know about dialysis, and was sure that I could fix the bone situation in Ottawa by using the techniques I'd learned in Montreal. I could not. The patients got worse. I was treating them the same way I'd been taught but they kept deteriorating, which made me suspect there must be something different in Ottawa. Could it be the water we were using for dialysis?

In those days, all haemodialysis units used ordinary tap water as the fluid to remove the toxins from the body. Tap water was being used in Montreal and Seattle and the patients did very well. We were using tap water in Ottawa but running into problems. I attended many medical conferences hoping to find an answer to Ottawa's bone disease troubles.

At the 1968 annual meeting of the ASAIO (the American Society for Artificial Internal Organs), Dr. Donald Tavis of Rochester, New York, presented a paper on fluoride in patients undergoing haemodialysis. He was worried about the possible side effects of the addition of fluoride to Rochester's municipal water. He postulated that it might cause a problem in haemodialysis and reach highly toxic levels because it might cross the dialyzing membrane and go into the blood. The membrane is what separates the blood from the fluid that removes the toxins. Dr. Tavis felt that if the toxins could go out across the membrane, then why couldn't elements not normally found in the body go the other way? He had measured fluoride in patients' blood before and after dialysis and had found that fluoride increased during dialysis.

That evening I was at a drug company–sponsored party and ran into Dr. Tavis. We discussed my patients' bone problems and the possible presence of toxins in Ottawa's water. Fluoride was added to Ottawa's water, which made me consider whether this might be the cause of our patients' problems. I knew that fluoride went into bone and that it was used medically as a drug to strengthen bones. But how could this element which strengthened bones weaken them? Could it have a deleterious effect on patients with renal failure on dialysis? Other drugs certainly do. And, though Ottawa was fluoridated at that time, neither Montreal nor Seattle were.

Dr. Tavis knew of John Marier, a researcher at the National Research Council in Ottawa, who was interested in fluoride. I contacted John, who was very interested in further pursuing fluoride and renal failure. He was involved with research in fluoride metabolism and thought that it could be contributing to the bone disease.

John suggested that I speak to a Professor Belanger, head of the department of histology at the University of Ottawa, who had done research on fluoride. Professor Belanger put me in touch with Dr. Frosst, a famous scientist in Washington, DC, who was also interested in fluoride. I traveled to Washington to meet him. He was quite excited about the problem and urged us to go further with our studies.

The more I read about fluoride and bone, the more it seemed that fluoride could be the problem. Investigating world literature, I discovered that although small doses of fluoride lead to dense, strong bone, there are exceptions. In India, for example, in areas where there are high levels of fluoride in the water and soil, people who were malnourished had bone disease similar to our patients. Our patients were on restricted diets; could chronic kidney failure act as malnourishment?

Donald Tavis, John Marier, and I had several meetings in Rochester and Ottawa to set up a study on my patients. We checked pre- and post-dialysis blood levels, and took bone biopsies and measured their fluoride. After we completed the study, but before the results were in, I decided to try to help my patients by dialyzing without fluoride.

One of my patients was Yvonne Lalonde, a young woman of eighteen who, within a year of starting dialysis, was in constant pain from her bone disease and was severely malnourished. At the time, the only way to get rid of the fluoride in the process was by using distilled or deionized water (water treated so that all the electrolyte particles are removed).

We found a small company in Hamilton, Ontario, that produced machinery to deionize water for laboratories and industry and they built us an enormous machine (ten feet high by twenty feet across) to provide us with enough pure water. Luckily, we had the space to set it up in our new haemodialysis unit so that we could dialyze all our patients. Sister Paquette, the head of the General Hospital, supported me. She believed in me and agreed to fund the deionizer, which was unproven but certainly would not harm the patients. Today, such a decision would require all sorts of committee approval.

Don, John, and I were thrilled to discover that when we used pure water the patients got better. Yvonne Lalonde, who had the most severe bone disease, immediately began to feel better after starting dialysis with pure water. Her appetite returned, and her bone pain improved and then disappeared entirely.

We ran into some opposition when we presented our data to the American Society of Nephrology in 1969. In fact, I was roundly criticized for implying that there might be problems with the water. However, the use of pure water for dialysis is now universally accepted.

(In 2009, I was invited to attend a special Kidney Foundation Dinner celebrating the fortieth anniversary of the year Yvonne

Lalonde, by then fifty-eight years old, had started dialysis. She'd had a kidney transplant in 1972 and she was very well. At the dinner she looked very beautiful, was happily married, and had children).

At that point, in 1968–69, I thought fluoride was causing the problem, but I wasn't positive. I made a very strong statement insisting that we should begin using pure water in dialysis. Later research showed it was the aluminum, not the fluoride, that was the culprit. It turned out that Ottawa water contained very high levels of aluminum that were caused by the pulp and paper industry. The industry uses aluminum that is then discharged into the Ottawa River, the source of our drinking water. Fortunately, purifying the water removed both the aluminum and fluoride.

* * *

There were still arguments concerning the presence of something in the water affecting our dialysis patients so, prior to treating patients, I took samples of their blood. That way, if we were wrong about fluoride and something else was being considered instead, I could just take out the samples and measure whatever it was. If the values of this new substance were high in the blood sample, it would help prove the substance in question was likely a problem.

I very carefully saved the samples in special containers so that they could not be contaminated and put the containers into the bottom of a freezer in the dialysis unit for safekeeping. I also stored samples of the water we were using. A year later, at an ASAIO meeting, someone gave a great paper on the possibility of tin being the problem in the water. I smiled to myself and thought, "I can answer that easily."

When I returned to Ottawa I ran straight to the freezer in the dialysis unit where I discovered, to my great chagrin, that the freezer was empty. All my precious samples of blood and water were gone. I ran to the head nurse – she was a wonderful nurse manager – and before I could say a word, she asked excitedly, "What do you think of the beautiful job I did cleaning out the freezer?"

And that was the end of the samples that might have made us very famous. They were thrown out in a cleaning purge.

As things turned out, neither tin nor fluoride were responsible; it was aluminum, which we could have measured in the samples. Unfortunately, it took a few more years for aluminum to be identified as the culprit. Had it not been for the cleaning of a freezer, I might have been famous. Ah well.

* * *

In January, 1969, in Vancouver, I presented our fluoride study to the Royal College of Physicians and Surgeons of Canada. The Canadian Press picked up the story and it became huge. Really huge. Articles on fluoride that suggested we had proved fluoridation of water was harmful to everyone appeared all over the world. In fact, we had shown only that the fluoride in water used for dialysis that went into patients could cause severe bone disease. We were careful not to say anything pro or con against fluoridation of city water.

Nonetheless, although incorrect, the genie was out of the bottle. We were in demand. We were invited to present the paper to the International Society for Fluoride Research at a meeting in Barcelona, Spain, which was held a day after the Vancouver meeting. I left Vancouver, flew home, got fresh clothes, boarded a plane to Barcelona, arrived, and went straight to the meeting. Almost as soon as I walked in I was called on to present. What a feeling! I was double jet-lagged, but I guess I went on nervous energy because the paper was very well received. (My luggage got lost in transit between Ottawa and Barcelona, but in those days things were cheap in Spain so I just bought new clothes.)

John Birch–types and other right-wingers tried to use our material as a major reason not to fluoridate, intimating that water was being poisoned with fluoride. While I was in Spain, the Canadian Dental Association attacked our work in general and me in particular for implying that fluoride – the tooth-saving wonder – might be a problem. When they couldn't find me, my nephrology colleagues at the General had to defend my work, although not all of them believed in it. I also received numerous letters from people around the world – one even comparing me to Jesus Christ. I never understood why.

I was forced to defend myself to make it understood that fluoride was just a potential toxin that only hurt patients on dialysis, and there was a way to remove it by using pure water in dialysis. At the time we didn't know that pure water also got rid of other substances.

John Lear, a science writer for *The Saturday Review of Literature*, became interested in the story and interviewed me on the phone for many hours at various times. He then published a series of three articles reviewing my work and the problems we'd had getting it published. His articles were actually quite fair. In our initial conversations he was very anti-fluoridation and felt we had proven the evils of it. In the end, he accepted the work for what it was and agreed that it was neither pro- nor anti-.

Locked up

As interns at MGH, we worked very hard; we put in extremely long hours on our many rotations. In addition, we were on call every second day and expected to put in a full day the day after. Little wonder friends who weren't doctors always commented on how tired I looked all that year. Since then, interns and residents have organized and formed unions so that now, in addition to receiving reasonable pay, they're on call one night in four and get the next day off.

In 1961, when I signed on to do my internship at the Montreal General Hospital, I was to be paid the princely sum of $45 per month. Fortunately, a few months before I started, the French residents in Montreal had gone on strike, and all the Montreal residents now benefited from a raise to $95 per month. It wasn't enough to live on, but since the hospital supplied room, board, laundry, and uniforms, all the money earned was for extras – as long as you weren't married.

There had been a mix-up when our living arrangements were assigned and instead of getting the usual single room, I wound up rooming with David Brattman, a first year resident in radiology. David had completed his internship in his native Ireland and come to Montreal to study the specialty of radiology. He'd arrived just the day before his residency started and was still in a state of advanced cultural shock.

Poor David. Whenever I was on call, the phone on the night table between us seemed to ring continuously. Radiologists were on call only once per week and even then they were rarely called at night. He learned to sleep without hearing the phone.

One Monday night, after I'd finished a weekend on duty, I suggested to David that we get dates and go downtown to a club that featured a sing-along pianist. I was totally exhausted, but loath to let my free time go to waste in that exciting city, and there were always nurses, graduates, or students happy to go out. David was up for it, so I called a nurse I knew who lived at the nurses' residence. She arranged a date for David and the four of us were off.

The hospital and the nurses' residence weren't far from downtown Montreal, so we walked to the club. We figured we could have a few drinks and calculated that, if we were very careful with our money, we'd be able to take a cab back to the hospital. Unfortunately, our good intentions went by the wayside. We spent every last nickel we had and realized, too late, that the four of us would have to walk home.

The evening had been great fun. We were all a little high-spirited, but not drunk because we'd had only enough money to buy two drinks apiece. David and I walked out of the club arm-in-arm singing at the top of our lungs. The girls, needless to say, pretended they didn't know us.

Suddenly, two cops materialized. "You're under arrest for creating a disturbance," they said. I couldn't believe they were serious. I explained that we were doctors at the Montreal General, that we'd been working very hard and apologized for any trouble. That seemed to trigger something inside them. "All you college kids are alike," they said. "You think you own the world. You're coming to the station with us." Fortunately, they left the girls alone. Everything happened so quickly that, before the girls realized what was going on, David and I had been thrown into the back of a squad car and spirited off.

David was beside himself. He was sure he was going to jail for life or – if he was lucky – he might only be deported. I thought the whole episode was a lark and I was sure it would be straightened out quickly.

If it wasn't, I had a big problem.

At the time, I was on a medical rotation where once a week Dr. Douglas Cameron, the chief of medicine, came to the ward to have one of the interns present a case to him. Dr. Cameron was very specific about what he wanted from his interns. In addition to insisting they know absolutely everything about the case – including the patient's family and work history – he expected they had also reviewed the latest literature on the subject.

We were all terrified of presenting. You really were under the microscope and all your colleagues were there to see how you did. I was well prepared for my presentation but concerned about getting to the ward on time. Tuesday was my day to present, and it was Monday night and I was about to wind up in jail.

The policemen took us to a small police station and put us in a holding cell. We were surrounded on all sides by bars just like in the movies. I took advantage of the opportunity to do something I'd wanted to do since the first time I'd seen a prison movie: I climbed all over those bars like they were monkey bars. Meanwhile, poor David sat in a corner worried stiff, terrified that he would be deported.

Suddenly, the cell doors opened and two well-dressed young fellows were escorted in. They were about our age – twenty-something – and they were having a good laugh. They told us they'd been arrested for breaking and entering but that the cops probably would have to let them go because they couldn't figure out what they had stolen. Then they shared their secret with us: they'd broken into a men's clothing store and were wearing – in layers – all the merchandise they'd lifted. A little while later they were let go for of lack of evidence.

The policemen didn't know what to do with David and me. They decided to send us off to the main police station to be held until morning when we'd be brought before a judge. We were stuffed into a paddy wagon with prostitutes, drunks, and robbers, and taken to the main station where we were put into a cage with the drunks.

It was still relatively early and already there wasn't a seat left in the cell. I foresaw a long night of standing. Then I had an idea. I was a smoker at the time and I said to David, "Watch what I do ... and be prepared to move." Then I took a few cigarettes from my pack and threw them into the middle of the floor. Mayhem ensued as our cellmates jumped out of their seats and jockeyed to get the cigarettes and as they scrambled over the floor David and I nabbed choice seats well away from the toilets.

As the night wore on I became increasingly worried about my upcoming presentation. I thought the whole misadventure was ridiculous and was sure the judge would throw it out. Then it occurred to me that if we could get bail or contact a lawyer, we might be able to get out of this mess and everything could be taken care of. I called a good friend at the hospital, brought him up to speed about our situation, and asked if he could provide bail. He was broke but was sure he could scrounge up the money from other friends. I told him to go for it but asked him to please keep mum about where we were.

About an hour later, Eli Rabin arrived at the police station in his hospital whites. Eli was a fellow intern, a brilliant guy who'd stood first in his class every year at Queen's University. He was laughing as he talked to us through the slot window. He'd been unable to raise any money for our bail, he said, but told me not to worry, he'd cover for me tomorrow with Dr. Cameron. He'd say I was ill, and no one would be any the wiser.

So we were stuck. What could I do? I befriended the man beside me. He seemed like a nice enough guy, though I found out he was in for beating his wife. Around 6:00 AM, breakfast was brought in by the Salvation Army. The deal was that you had to sing hymns to get breakfast. As a good Jewish boy, I refused – so it looked like there'd be no breakfast for me. Luckily, my friend the wife-beater took pity on me and brought me something to eat.

About mid-morning we were taken into court and when the judge heard the charges he was furious. He called David and me to the bench and asked us whether, in fact, that was our story. We assured him that we hadn't been drunk, just happy, and we'd been working at the hospital without sleep for a long time. He immediately dismissed all charges and ordered everything removed from the record. He apologized for the police and sent us on our way.

Back at the hospital David went straight to bed. I showered, put on my hospital whites and ran to the ward. I arrived just as Eli finished my presentation. I tried to be unobtrusive, but as soon as they spotted me Dr. Cameron and the others laughed and had a great time teasing me about my night in jail.

Fortunately, there were no sequels to the incident. But it became a famous story that's probably still circulating among interns to this day.

David never double-dated with me after that and the girls never went out with me again. Eli and I remained very close friends but I never completely forgave him. When I was made chief of nephrology at the Ottawa Civic Hospital, I brought him to Ottawa to work with me.

The heart of the matter

On one of my first rotations in medicine, our team – a resident, a senior resident, two junior residents, two interns, and two medical students – was making rounds with our staff man when suddenly the patient we were with had a cardiac arrest before our eyes. Out of nowhere, I heard my voice ordering my colleagues to get the patient on the floor and instructing them on how to proceed.

The whole team, especially the staff man, was incredulous but, in between compressing the patient's chest, I explained that we were administering closed cardiac massage, a brand new technique for sudden stoppage of the heart. Purely by happenstance I was the only team member aware of the technique because just the night before I'd read about it in the latest issue of the *New England Journal of Medicine*.

At the time, the only known method was open cardiac massage, which required cutting open the patient's chest and compressing the heart in your hand to maintain blood flow until the heart started again. Unfortunately, that method had a very high failure rate and, even when successful, almost always was associated with infection. The *Journal* article showed closed cardiac massage to be equally as effective and without surgery.

In closed cardiac massage, the chest compression was administered with the patient lying on a hard surface. This procedure kept blood flowing to vital organs without the trauma that opening the chest cage caused.

Unfortunately, our patient's heart did not restart, but the merit of the method was immediately obvious. The technique quickly became routine and is still in use.

None of my colleagues had seen the article because, inexplicably, my copy of the *Journal* had arrived a day early.

* * *

One situation I came across in Espanola involved a difficult elderly woman with severe arthritis who made no effort to get out of her wheelchair and ruled over her family like a tyrant. She was on aspirin, at the time the only drug that worked for arthritis.

One day the woman's family brought her to the hospital's emergency room. She was in very bad shape but still behaving in her usual tenacious fashion. She was complaining of stomach pain and was also in heart failure. Her legs were swollen and large. I knew that she was on aspirin for arthritis and, since aspirin can cause many stomach problems, among them bleeding ulcers, I decided to check for stomach ulcers.

I arranged with the X-ray technician to do a barium swallow to see if there was an ulcer there. The procedure requires the patient to be put on a table that can incline, thus affording the doctor different views. The technician raised the patient's head and body to the vertical position but before he could give her the barium to swallow, the woman clutched her chest and had a cardiac arrest. I tried to resuscitate her but I was unsuccessful.

I think what caused the cardiac arrest was that, as soon as the patient was vertical, she threw a large blood clot to her lungs.

THE HEART OF THE MATTER

Since she had not walked or been upright for years and had been sitting in a wheelchair with her knees bent, a thrombosis was bound to occur.

* * *

One day I was summoned to the emergency room to see a patient with severe chest pain. When I got to the ER I found a big man – six feet tall, weighing at least three-hundred pounds, looking very grey – on the table clutching his chest.

I examined the patient and was listening to his heart when it just stopped. I couldn't feel a pulse. I immediately realized that he'd gone into ventricular fibrillation and knew I had to resuscitate him by starting closed cardiac massage and then defibrillate him.

Although his heart had stopped, he was still conscious, so I told him to get off the table and get onto the floor. He got up, lay down on the floor, and instantly went unconscious. We tried to resuscitate him but unfortunately it was unsuccessful.

I've often wondered what that patient's last thoughts might have been. Why was this crazy doctor telling him to get off the table and lie down on the floor? The reason was that he was so very large that I couldn't resuscitate him on that small examining table. And I certainly couldn't have gotten him onto the floor by myself.

* * *

During my time on rotation in Charlotte, I became quite fond of a patient who was in my care. He was a very interesting individual who had come in with an acute heart attack and gone on to do very well. The day he was being discharged I went to wish him good luck and give him the usual instructions. We chatted for a few minutes longer and then he said, "Thank you very much. I appreciate everything you did for me." We parted company, he went on his way, and I continued making my rounds on the ward.

I was in a patient's room when a nurse came running in. "Dr. Posen, Mr. X really wants to see you," she said. "He said it's very important and asked if you could get to him quickly."

I immediately went to see the gentleman, who looked at me and said, "Dr. Posen, I just want to tell you again how thankful I am for all you've done for me." Then he made a guttural noise in his throat and died right before my eyes! I tried to resuscitate him but I was unsuccessful. He obviously had a premonition that something was about to happen and had wanted to say something to me.

* * *

Recently, Josée and I purchased a condo in a gated community in Florida where we happily park ourselves for the winter months. We're enjoying it tremendously.

After I retired I learned to play bridge and it has become a pleasurable pastime for me in Ottawa and in Florida. Occasionally, even at a bridge game, I get to put my medical training to use, like the afternoon when I was deeply ensconced in duplicate bridge at the club near our condo.

In duplicate bridge, one pair – the north/south partnership – remains stationary while the other pair – the east/west partnership – plays three hands and moves on to the next table. On that afternoon, a good friend was playing with an older gent named

Jerry. When it was time to move, I heard shouting. "Jerry, move! Jerry, move!" I looked around me and, two tables over, there was an elderly gentleman leaning forward – eyes staring straight ahead, oblivious to all the shouting. I realized something more was happening and I ran over to find him sitting up, unconscious. I checked his pulse and it was very irregular and weak. I got him to the floor and his pulse stopped. I began administering closed cardiac massage. His pulse came back gradually and he started to regain consciousness. What was so utterly amazing was that all around us not only did everyone keep playing bridge but they didn't even move to allow me room. As I administered and organized help with cardiac resuscitation I had to get people to move their tables and chairs to clear an area for the paramedics. The players listened, but grumpily. By the time the paramedics arrived there was lots of room and the other Jerry was conscious and complaining of chest pain.

The paramedics got the fellow to the hospital where he was diagnosed with a heart attack and resulting arrhythmia, which caused his heart to stop. He discharged himself the next day and returned to the bridge club as if nothing happened. He remembered nothing of the episode. Once an active doctor, always an active doctor, although I am officially retired and have given up my licence.

Fighting panic

June, 1960. I had just finished my third year of medical school. Only one more year to go.

In those days medical students were not allowed to assume any clinical responsibility until their fourth and final year. Now that I was about to enter my final year I took a summer job as an extern at St. Thomas Elgin General Hospital. St. Thomas is a small town approximately thirty kilometres south of London, Ontario. I was to spend one month doing medicine and one month doing surgery.

In a small hospital an extern acts as an intern. That is, they spend all day in the hospital and take night call in rotation, but live outside the hospital. When on call, the extern stays in the hospital in a duty room outfitted with a bed, a bathroom, and a telephone. Every third night it was my turn to be on call for the whole hospital. Whenever problems arose at night the nurses always called the extern first. If the extern couldn't handle the problem or needed advice, he or she called the patient's physician or the on-call physician who was at home but easily obtainable.

One night I was called in to see an elderly male patient who was severely short of breath. I grabbed my book of therapeutics and ran to the ward, where I found the poor man drowning in his own fluid. I could see the gentleman was in extreme distress and likely would die if I didn't do something, and fast. I had never encountered this situation before but I knew it definitely couldn't wait for the on-call physician.

Fortunately, I remembered the description of the condition from class and correctly diagnosed acute pulmonary edema, a condition due to heart failure that can be rapidly fatal. The patient develops severe anxiety because he can't catch his breath and feels as if he is drowning. Fortunately, too, I also remembered the therapy. As soon as I started treatment – oxygen and some intravenous morphine – the patient calmed down. After the remainder of the therapy was administered he was perfectly normal and breathing easy. By the time the staff physician arrived the patient and I were laughing and joking together.

Bringing a man from near death to laughter was a very emotional moment for me. It was incredibly gratifying to witness such a dramatic improvement. In that moment I knew why I had chosen to go into medicine.

Today, medical students are on the wards earlier – in second year, in fact – and have responsibilities under resident supervision in their third and fourth years. Because they take call with resident supervision, they would see this and many other types of cases in the emergency room and would be well-trained to deal with them.

* * *

On my second night on call I was on a ward when the loud speaker blared, "Dr. Posen to emergency. *Stat.*" It was an automobile accident. Four ambulances had had to pick up the injured and were on their way to the hospital.

There I was, a real neophyte, all alone with a major emergency unfolding. I reached the on-call staff doctors and they informed me they were en route, but I knew the ambulances would arrive before they did. Never in my life, before or since, have I experienced such a strong feeling of panic; I wished I could run away. I kept telling myself to stop panicking. I kept repeating the emergency dictum: *Stop Bleeding and Keep Breathing. Stop Bleeding and Keep Breathing.*

Fortunately, a very experienced nurse was in emergency with me. Between the two of us we got everything organized and had the patients stabilized by the time the staff physicians came in. No one died and everyone got taken care of, but never in my life have I been as happy to see anyone as I was to see the first staff man walk in.

I shook when it was all over. The emergency room nurse had been great. It had not been her first time handling the aftermath of an accident with a neophyte doctor, and we'd worked well together. The staff physician was very impressed. But, in all honesty, it was the very competent nurse who did what had to be done with help from me, and not the other way around.

That was a very important learning experience for me. First, I learned that I could control my panic and force myself to think clearly; second, and most important, I learned that sometimes you have to solve a problem very quickly.

* * *

Like all the interns, I worked very hard. I was on call every second or third night and often got little sleep. When I did sleep, I slept very soundly.

One night, I got a very late call – about 3:00 AM – from a nurse on the ward. She was concerned about an elderly man who couldn't pass urine and required a urinary catheter placed in his bladder to relieve the obstruction. In those days nurses weren't permitted to catheterize a patient.

I was so terribly tired and through my sleepy haze I said I'd be up to look after it in the morning. But when I tried to go back to sleep I developed sympathy pains with the patient. My own bladder became so uncomfortable that I realized I just couldn't let him be. I got up, went to the ward, put in the catheter, returned to bed, and promptly fell back into a deep sleep.

* * *

I was covering emergency as the senior resident at Baltimore City Hospital when a severe snowstorm hit, dropping almost a metre of snow. The emergency entrance was located approximately one kilometre from the main road and the road leading to the emergency was unplowed. Ambulance drivers were carrying the patients through the deep snow on foot.

Two ambulance drivers, not huge men, brought in a woman who weighed at least three-hundred pounds. The duo managed to get her onto a table, almost collapsing in the process. They had carried her all the way in from the main road and were justifiably proud that they had saved her life and had not dropped her or set her down.

I examined the woman and found nothing very serious. In truth, there was no reason at all for her to be in the hospital, but I waited until the exhausted ambulance attendants left the hospital before I discharged her. I don't know how she got home. I suspect she probably had to wait in the waiting room all day before the road was plowed and cabs could get through.

I've learned over the years how very dedicated most of the medical and ancillary hospital staff are.

Haemodialysis

My car, an old Nash Metropolitan, was giving me trouble. It was always acting up and rarely started during the winter. So I decided to dip into my savings, go into debt, and buy a brand new sports car. I chose a Triumph TR4. It was a beauty – a white convertible with red upholstery (a chick magnet). The nurses loved it.

With the end of our internship at MGH approaching, Eli Rabin and I arranged our holidays so that we had two extra weeks off – six weeks in total. We planned to drive to California and have a good time.

About six weeks before we were scheduled to leave, Dr. Kaye asked us if we we'd consider giving up those extra two weeks, rearrange the remainder of our holiday time, and take consecutive months off separately. He needed help: his renal fellow was going to Washington with her husband and he wanted our assistance with a patient with acute renal failure who was not improving. The patient was being kept alive by the artificial kidney machine and a doctor had to be present for each treatment.

In 1962, the artificial kidney machine and haemodialysis were very new. The artificial kidney is a device that temporarily replaces the function of the human kidneys. Haemodialysis is the process of cleansing the blood by filtering out the toxins as the blood flows through an artificial kidney.

Dr. Kaye had one of the first dialysis machines in Canada and it was being used primarily for renal failure that would get better. Unfortunately, although Dr. Kaye's patient had been on treatment twice per week, he showed no sign of improving, no sign that his own kidneys were getting better. This meant he would have to continue with dialysis (artificial kidney therapy) for the rest of his life.

Neither Eli nor I knew anything about the artificial kidney, but we were eager to learn so we agreed to stay. We knew that being involved in this case would be exciting and that we'd be in at the start of something groundbreaking. I couldn't know then that making that decision would change my life, lead to a career in nephrology and haemodialysis, and result in my being considered one of the pioneers of Canadian dialysis.

Dr. Kaye taught us how to set up and run the artificial kidney machine. His patient, a thirty-three-year-old man, had developed acute glomerulonephritis (an inflammation of the kidneys, not an infection) and had stopped putting out urine. Other than undergoing haemodialysis, there was no other treatment available for the condition. The patient's only option was to be careful of his fluid intake – drink no more than the equivalent of two glasses of water per day – and follow a diet restricted in protein, salt, and potassium. All he could do was diet and wait for the condition to improve. If it didn't, he would die. It was as simple as that.

Dr. Kaye's patient became the first chronic haemodialysis patient in Canada. Eli and I took over his care in mid-June. We treated him for four or five hours per day, twice per week, and had to stay right there with him.

The apparatus was very complicated and each treatment required four units of fresh blood from the blood bank. That amounted to a lot of blood and a lot of work for the blood bank, but with their cooperation and the cooperation of many other departments in the hospital (and huge expenses for the equipment, tubing, saline, nurses, and the blood bank itself), we continued.

That first artificial kidney came with several problems, one of which was attaching the device to the patient's blood circulation. At the time, the only available means for connection was a plastic tube that was surgically inserted into a large blood vessel in the arm or leg. Unfortunately, the tubes only worked for a few days. Then, if the patient didn't get better, when there were no good blood vessels left for connection to the blood stream, he or she died of kidney failure.

Eli and I got to know the patient very well; we became friends. We hoped and prayed that he'd get better. He was such a young man and had three children at home. As his treatment progressed, he was alive but not doing well. His blood results were good but there were many other things that were still unknown at the time. When he didn't improve, we kept trying different ways of connecting to the artificial kidney until we were out of options, left with no means of dialyzing him. Ultimately, he died. Not, however, while he was undergoing dialysis. His death was very, very emotional for Eli and me. We sat in the intern's lounge, utterly devastated.

There still remained much to be discovered concerning haemodialysis: the access and the use of blood, the electrolyte solutions, and the monitoring of the procedure. Eli and I together – and then alone – would setup the apparatus, prime the coils with blood, attach the patient, and make up the bath with powdered electrolytes and tap water. A nurse worked with us, but her only role was checking the patient's blood pressure. Today, the nurses attach the patient to the dialysis machine and then monitor the patients. Today, too, everything is automated and one nurse with nursing assistants can look after many patients.

By the time I was a nephrology resident, dialysis had changed considerably. The new coils were smaller and didn't need extra blood. Two Seattle doctors – Drs. Scribner and Quinton – had invented the shunt, which allowed a patient to be dialyzed for an indefinite period of time and even to do the treatment at home.

* * *

One evening, I was at the hospital working late – not an unusual occurrence – when I was paged to the dialysis room, *urgent*. I was working at a desk in the renal unit, which was on the sixth floor, and the dialysis unit was on the tenth floor. I raced up the stairs and into the unit to discover that all the blood leaving the haemodialyzer had turned brown – and the blood pressure of the patients being dialyzed was falling.

I realized immediately that the blood was being haemolyzed (that the red cells, which carry oxygen, were being destroyed) and the patients were becoming hypoxic (not receiving oxygen) and in danger of dying. I ordered all the dialysis stopped; no blood was to go to the dialyzers. Four patients were being dialyzed at the same time using a common dialysate bath, so I instructed the nurses to start oxygen and saline infusions in all four. Three responded quickly with a rise in their blood pressure. But the fourth patient's blood pressure remained low – so low that when we attempted to check his haemoglobin we couldn't measure it. I gave him additional saline and oxygen and we managed to keep him alive until fresh blood arrived from the blood bank. Then he settled down and did fine.

It was 1963, in the very early days of haemodialysis, and the question was: what had caused this? The head of nephrology, Dr. Kaye, had designed a system that allowed us to dialyze four patients at once. The system worked on the principle that toxins could be passed through the artificial kidney membrane into the common dialysis bath and the electrolytes in the bath could go into each patient. This method was developed to save money, because there was no funding for chronic dialysis at that time.

The bath was made up of various components that were added to the solution prior to starting the treatment. It seems incredible now, but in those early days we didn't bother to double-check to see that all the components had been added, we just assumed they were. When we checked this bath, we discovered that a package of sodium chloride had been left out. Without going into details of the chemistry, the omission of salt in the solution caused severe haemolysis, or destruction, of red blood cells. We were very lucky every one of the patients survived. Following that close call, a rule was instituted requiring staff to sign as they placed each individual powder into the bath fluid, and we managed to find money to buy a gauge that measured the accuracy of the concentration of ions.

In the early 1960s, the dialysis equipment was very primitive. It was difficult to get the funds to dialyze patients. Hospitals run on budgets, and haemodialysis wasn't in the budget then.

We were very proud of our system because, despite occasional challenges, it did work effectively and was relatively inexpensive to run. We subsequently presented it to a nephrology meeting, but were outdone by Seattle's Dr. Belding Scribner and his group. Dr. Scribner was the brilliant nephrologist who also solved the problem of access to the circulation for chronic haemodialysis. His group was way ahead of us. They presented a different approach to chronic haemodialysis, and their patients fared much better than ours. Following that meeting, we returned to Montreal and quickly changed to the Seattle approach – with the result that our patients improved, had fewer complications, and lived longer.

* * *

Until 1964, haemodialysis was done exclusively in hospital. But that year, nephrologists in Seattle, under the guidance of Dr. Scribner, created the world's first home haemodialysis program and, for some patients, the venue changed.

Once the University of Seattle developed its program, machinery that simplified the treatment was developed and numerous safeguards were built into the system. The spouses and friends of patients who qualified for home haemodialysis were taught how to do the procedure and physicians, nurses, and technicians were on call 24/7 to help with problems. In short order, many patients all over North America were being treated at home and doing very well.

Dr. Michael Kaye introduced the first home haemodialysis program to Canada in 1966 at the Montreal General Hospital. I was working with him and was tremendously impressed at how well patients did and how well they felt. His design was a very simple but effective system that was inexpensive to build. We had no money so the device was unbelievably primitive – but it worked. The cost factor was very important in 1966 because there was little money for haemodialysis available from governments, and none at all earmarked for home dialysis.

Two years later, as a young nephrologist at the Ottawa General Hospital, I felt we should introduce home dialysis to Ottawa. I had seen how well patients did in Montreal and felt we could do it in Ottawa, too. If we succeeded, it would be only the second home haemodialysis program available in Canada.

However, I felt that Seattle's home dialysis program was superior to Montreal's, so I arranged to go to Seattle to learn what I could about their methods and machinery. Seattle's machinery was safer, less time consuming, and easier to set up for the patient. Their machine was produced by Drake Willock, a Seattle company, and designed with the input of University of Seattle nephrologists. I spent an invaluable week in Seattle with Dr. Scribner and Dr. Joseph Eschbach, gaining an appreciation of the tremendous advantages of home dialysis and how to do it.

Seattle operated its home dialysis program out of a motel located near the hospital and it was proving very effective because, in the non-hospital setting, patients felt less like ailing patients. The neutral environment helped them adapt to home haemodialysis readily and they did exceptionally well. Drs. Scribner and Eschbach were also working with patients from across the United States and around the world and their patients were doing better than any dialysis patients I had ever seen. I was sure we could do this in Ottawa.

When I got back to Ottawa, I set up a home dialysis program in the General Hospital in a room off our new main unit, but I hoped to follow Seattle and run the program outside the hospital. As luck had it, a little while later an apartment became available in a building owned by the hospital some three blocks away and we set up our own home dialysis unit.

At the outset, there was no money. But then, as the result of the sudden death of one of my home dialysis patients, funds became available. The patient, a Mr. Gerard Lemay, who was severely wounded in World War II, had been very active in the War

Amps association. When he died, the War Amps established a fund in his memory and donated funds from it to furnish our apartment. We named the unit the Gerard Lemay Home Dialysis Unit. Then, another patient, Choo Leung, the restauranteur who often had helped us when there was a need, donated air conditioners, and another, Lorne Murphy, donated TV sets. We were off and running. The unit opened in 1969 and soon was serving approximately forty home haemodialysis patients in eastern and even northern Ontario.

The first machines we used were similar to the apparatus used by Dr. Kaye in Montreal, until I discovered that service clubs – Kiwanis, Lions, Rotary – would help us purchase machines similar to those used in Seattle. I got in touch with them, explained what was needed, and was invited to speak at their meetings. I used to begin my remarks by joking that I would sing for my supper. Each machine cost about $4,000 to $5,000, and each club presented me a cheque sufficient to pay for one machine.

The ongoing costs of the unit came out of our general haemodialysis budget, thanks to Sister Paquette and the Sisters of Charity (the Grey Nuns), who owned and ran the Ottawa General Hospital. The Sisters and I had an excellent relationship and helped me in many ways that would not be possible today. I had three patients who were being treated at home, and was able to scrounge money to cover the costs, including the machinery.

I was president of the Nephrology Section of the Ontario Medical Association (OMA) at the time we initiated the home haemodialysis program in Ottawa. My vice president, Dr. Art Shimizu, had trained with Dr. Kaye a year after me and had set up a home dialysis program in Hamilton supported by the Catholic Sisters at St. Joseph's Hospital. Art and I got an appointment with Dr. Matthew Dymond, the Ontario health minister, through the

OMA. We prepared a thorough cost breakdown hoping to persuade him that treating a patient at home was much less costly than in hospital, and that patients felt much better and could live a more normal life. The minister told us he was persuaded mainly by the well-being of the patients and Ontario became the first province in Canada to fund home haemodialysis totally. The funding included the cost of refitting the patient's home to accommodate the system and, where required, drilling wells in the countryside when extra water was needed for the system. I was very proud of our provincial government.

The majority of our patients were from Ottawa and its environs but we did have a few who weren't from the area. One, a Venezuelan woman, was the wife of a diplomat. When her husband's Ottawa posting was over and he was recalled to Venezuela, we arranged for the dialysis machinery to be moved to Venezuela and we continued to monitor her. She called us whenever a problem cropped up and flew up to see me every two or three months until haemodialysis got established in Venezuela and doctors there took over her care.

When a woman from Chapleau, Ontario, northwest of Sudbury, learned she'd require dialysis for many years she was beside herself because it meant she'd have to move to Ottawa; there were no dialysis facilities near her. Needless to say, she was thrilled when she heard about home dialysis. She was an excellent pupil and lived for many years on home dialysis. She used to come in to see us every three months and, of course, called whenever she ran into a situation and needed help.

Another patient was a man in the air force who was stationed at North Bay. The air force kept him on despite his kidney problems because he wasn't a pilot and did his particular job very well. We taught his wife and him to run the system, although usually he was able to do it all himself. He used to haemodialyze at night and this arrangement worked so well that he was able to work during the day, missing very little time. Eventually he had a successful kidney transplant.

All in all, the program ran exceptionally well. It was set up as a regional program and has remained so. At its height we were following approximately forty patients on haemodialysis in homes all over Ontario, and one in Venezuela. Civic Hospital patients received their training in home haemodialysis at the Ottawa General Hospital.

In time, our home haemodialysis patient load began to decrease mainly because of the development of CAPD (chronic ambulatory peritoneal dialysis). CAPD was also a form of home dialysis which was much simpler to teach and much easier to learn than haemodialysis. As one of my nurses used to say, "If you can make a cup of tea, you can do CAPD."

In peritoneal dialysis, the lining of the abdomen (the peritoneum) is used as the membrane for toxin removal. Fluid is placed in the abdomen by a catheter that goes through the skin into the abdominal cavity. The fluid is then left there for four to six hours before being removed. After the fluid is injected, the patients are disconnected from the external bags in which the fluid is delivered. People can then act normally: walk, sleep, go out, even work. It is equally as effective as haemodialysis and many patients prefer it. Its advantage is the ease of training and safety because of its lack of connection to the blood stream.

The program, which still exists, moved to the new General Hospital in 1980 with all other programs at the old Ottawa General. Since 2002, the program has been operating at the Riverside Campus of The Ottawa Hospital in an outpatient clinic–like atmosphere separate from the main haemodialysis units. It now services many patients on peritoneal dialysis, home haemodialysis, and nocturnal haemodialysis.

* * *

At a meeting of the American Society of Nephrology, Dr. Emil Paganini presented a paper about a new treatment for acute renal failure in difficult patients. I invited him to Ottawa and he presented his work in great detail. He taught us how to use the procedure. It involved blood continuously flowing slowly from the body into a filter, then back into the body. The treatment was continuous: we could adjust the fluid intake and calorie intake easily and rid the body of toxins. This was more like the normal kidney, which is always working.

I was interested in the new procedure. At that time, when the cardiac surgery unit operated on very difficult patients, blood pressure in some cases remained low after the operations and this led to kidney failure. Our results with the regular treatment of intermittent dialysis in these severe post–cardiac surgery patients was very poor: about 80 percent of the patients did not recover and died. With the introduction of this new treatment, 90 percent of these renal failure patients survived. It is a technique, though greatly modified, which is still used in the ICU in very sick patients with renal failure.

* * *

The home haemodialysis unit that I initiated was working well. All the patients lived in Ontario, save the Venezuelan patient who had entered the program while resident in Ottawa and who had now returned to South America. The fact that all the patients were Ontarians was important, because my funding came from Ontario. The province of Quebec, on the other hand, had refused to pay for home dialysis, a circumstance that created a problem when we received a patient referral from Pembroke, Ontario.

The problem was that the patient, Mr. Laperriere, was in end-stage renal failure and needed dialysis, but he lived on the Quebec side of the Ottawa River, directly across from Pembroke. We could arrange for him to be dialyzed in The Ottawa Hospital but it was too long a distance for him to be traveling three times per week, which was precisely why we had instituted home dialysis.

His daughter was a nurse who worked at the Pembroke General Hospital. She was willing to learn how to dialyze her father at his home but, because he lived in Quebec, we couldn't get funding for it. Then I had a thought: if we could appropriate a room at the Pembroke General Hospital and we could get funding to equip it for dialysis, his daughter could dialyze him there on her off time. It would be a true satellite unit, probably the first in Canada, possibly even in the world. Today, satellite units that are supplied and run by major hospitals are common.

I brought my idea to the Sister who was the head of the Pembroke General Hospital. She agreed and assigned a room off of the emergency room. We used it for Mr. Laperriere and for another patient from the Renfrew, Ontario, area in need of chronic dialysis. The second patient's wife was able to assist him. Other than the operation itself, all supplies came from the Ottawa General Hospital.

Mr. Laperriere ran a small farm. He had a few horses and had us out to his farm, where he introduced us to a very gentle pony named Candy. Then, he presented us with Candy as a gift. My sons, Dan and Andy, were thrilled, but I insisted on paying for the pony; I felt it was wrong to accept the gift.

That little pony changed our lives. We bought a cart for him; he was a very strong animal and great at pulling. Andy would ski behind him by attaching a rope to the saddle while Dan rode Candy. At first we found a stable a kilometre or two from our house, but soon we wound up buying a hobby farm outside of Stittsville, a small community to the west of Ottawa, that had chickens and horses. We lived there for nine years and actually ran the farm. We enjoyed that pony and the many friends we met through the stable.

Statistics and more statistics

In 1975, Dr. Art Shimizu, my good friend and colleague from Hamilton, created a registry of all Ontario patients on dialysis. By having a record of every patient who was on dialysis in Ontario one could measure the number of new patients entering dialysis, the types of diseases that caused renal failure, how long people lived on dialysis, their age, sex, and many more facts that would help both physicians and governments plan for the future. In time, Art expanded the registry to cover all of Canada. While the concept was excellent, neither the provincial nor the federal registry ever worked well because nephrology units neglected to send in their data or reports and, even when they finally did, they were often three or four years late.

Understandably, Art was disappointed and frustrated, but he still felt strongly that it was worthwhile continuing. One day he approached me to ask if I would take over the registry. When I told him I knew nothing about running a registry, he confided that he had a second choice in mind – another colleague – someone with whom I didn't get along. I gave the matter serious thought, reconsidered, and agreed to undertake the registry.

And then I discovered the registry was virtually dead.

No reports of findings had been written for three years, no data had been analyzed for three years, and there was no money available to do anything with the data that had been sent in.

Nonetheless, I believed with Art that having a registry was an excellent idea and believed the data from a well-functioning registry was essential both for government planning and for physicians' understanding of what was happening in the field.

There was a lot of interest in reorganizing the registry. The original attempt had been funded by the Kidney Foundation of Canada and Statistics Canada, the government statistics agency.

Fortunately, this time around we had Fred Coll. Fred was a patient of the Ottawa General Hospital who happened to be on the executive of the Kidney Foundation. He was also a former bureaucrat, very intelligent, and terrifically organized. Fred realized that a registry was critical for government planning and financing. If I'd agree to be the medical director, he said he would find funds to run it. Fred eventually worked out a deal with Health Canada, Statistics Canada, and the Kidney Foundation of Canada to have each supply one third of the necessary start-up funds. The original budget was $60,000, with each party contributing $20,000 to the pot.

Since the nephrology community would have to put in the data, we needed their approval. I made a presentation to the council of the Canadian Society of Nephrology (CSN) explaining that I'd reorganize the registry to make it simpler, and produce reports within three months of the end of each yearly cycle. I also agreed to assume the position of medical director if I alone could set up the committees and determine the questions. (Art had been saddled with a committee that made everything very complicated). After many arguments, the council agreed, and I became medical director of the Canadian Renal Failure Register.

But I really needed to know more about running a registry. The largest and most successful organization of this type was the European Dialysis and Transplant Registry in London, England, so I wrote to its head, Dr. Tony Wing, who invited me to visit him in London. I spent a week with him and his advice was invaluable.

Dr. Wing told me to keep things simple – to register deceased patients only by age, sex, renal diagnosis, type of therapy, and date of death. Since all new patients would be registered, it would be easy to obtain material from the units. We would also get data from each unit on patient numbers, the breakdown of patients on different therapies, the number of new patients, and the number of deaths. Again, nothing complicated. To prove the usefulness of the registry, Dr. Wing also suggested that I deliver an early report showing trends. I arranged for the doctor to come and speak about the European Registry to the CSN. He gave an excellent talk and helped convince the group that this time around it was for real.

The registry lucked in when we hired a data clerk who had worked as a librarian at the National Institutes of Health in Washington, DC. She was especially good at chasing down all the units. We couldn't afford to pay large sums to the units for providing us with their data but we did arrange to pay $2 per form for each patient they registered.

All the data came in to Statistics Canada. My colleagues and I met at StatsCan weekly and continued to meet until 1987, when I stepped down as medical director. (The registry has since been replaced by the Canadian Organ Replacement Register (CORR), which oversees all organ transplants in Canada). My aim was to have every unit across Canada submit its data to the registry so that I could give the first report at the CSN meeting, and deliver the final report within the next calendar year.

Some units didn't send their data. I dealt with that problem by calling nephrologists at each of the truant units and telling a little white lie – that they were the only unit in the country whose data hadn't been sent in. I succeeded in getting material from nine of the ten delinquents. When it came to the final hold-out, I had an ace up my sleeve. Its head of medicine had been my resident as an intern in Montreal. I called, told him the problem I was having with his head of dialysis and, one-two-three, the outstanding data arrived. We achieved 100 percent participation from across Canada.

The CSN meeting took place in Quebec City. All the material that was given out was bilingual and, as we had promised, we presented data from the first six months of the new registry. Everyone was pleased: the material was both timely and very useful. I commissioned my cousin's wife, who is French, to translate a summary into French so I could deliver my presentation in both French and English. Her written French was accurate but my accent was, to say the least, wanting; the spoken words were almost impossible to understand. The effort proved worthwhile, however, because for the six years I was medical director we always had the full participation of all the units, both French and English.

Our publication, The Canadian Renal Failure Register, was ready in the next calendar year. It consisted of sixty-five pages and was completely paid for through the sale of advertising space to dialysis and drug companies. All the haemodialysis units and nephrologists in the country received it.

During my years as medical director of the registry I published papers and presented Canadian data all over the world. It was a very exciting time for me. I was invited to attend a meeting in Dallas at which registries from all over the world had been invited to present data. The results of that meeting changed the way dialysis was done and is still referred to as a groundbreaking event. I considered myself fortunate to be part of it. I worked with excellent people from Statistics Canada – John Sillins, Eric Lam, Anna Malahotra, Luling Mao, Daniel Lucas, and Anita Rapaport (our data clerk) – with whom I discussed where we were going, how to improve, and what to publish.

Suing the minister of health

About twenty years into my career, I realized dialysis units should be of two kinds. The first: in-hospital, to dialyze those patients who require hospitalization or are too unstable during dialysis to be treated anywhere else. The second: a non-hospital setting where "well" patients could be dialyzed in a separate facility away from the hospital (moreover, dialyzing in a non-hospital setting should be less costly to run). I felt that being treated in hospital makes patients – especially patients who are coping well and functioning normally – feel they are sick. The idea was not original; it had already been done successfully in the US.

I tried – unsuccessfully – to set up meetings with people in government to get the ball rolling on this second type of care. I even talked to people from Baxter Corporation, a large dialysis company, and they were interested in pursuing it. But in 1980, the Ontario government was not yet interested.

During the six years I ran the Canadian Renal Failure Register, I attended many meetings at which I presented Canadian data. At these meetings I'd been very impressed by presentations made by National Medical Care (NMC), a large US company. NMC owned and operated over a thousand dialysis units in the US and in England. Their presentations were particularly important because they used data from their own units and demonstrated some very good research.

I decided to approach NMC about setting up similar units in Canada. NMC was interested, and we met to try to adapt the American model to the Canadian situation. We managed to work out quite a reasonable scheme that basically involved setting up a not-for-profit corporation, all the funding for which would come from the Ontario government. The company would make its money through management fees. We decided that I would be the medical director and run the units according to standards of practice in Canada.

We approached the Ontario government but still they weren't interested. However, not long afterwards, there was a public outcry protesting the lack of dialysis facilities in Ontario. The government responded by putting out a request for proposals for new dialysis centres. We were prepared and, in conjunction with NMC, put forward two proposals, for a unit in Ottawa and a unit in Cornwall.

We heard nothing for a several months. Then a problem surfaced: the *New York Times* published an expose on NMC, accusing them of numerous misdemeanours in their dialysis units. The accusations appeared on the front page of the *Times* for three successive days. I figured we were finished as far as our joint proposal went. And, just to be sure the government heard about it before they made their decision, I called the assistant deputy minister (ADM) of health of Ontario. We knew each other from when I was president of the OMA section on nephrology, and from when I ran the registry. I had also worked with him on various dialysis-related topics over the years. "We've all read the *Times* articles, Jerry," the ADM said. "It doesn't look good for your proposal."

I was quite discouraged, but when NMC put out a defence that the *Times* published, I decided to fax all the material to the ministry. That way, no matter what happened, I could not be accused of failing to notify the government. In fact, I faxed the material to the minister of health, the deputy minister, the assistant deputy minister, the head of the dialysis programs for the province, and gave a copy to the head of the Ottawa Civic Hospital. I also made very sure to keep the records verifying that the faxes had been sent to and received by the all departments to which they were addressed.

Several months passed without incident until the government announced the licensing of dialysis units in southern and central Ontario. No mention was made of eastern Ontario. Then, one day, I received a call from a secretary in the Ontario government advising me that a press conference would be held in one week at which an announcement would be made concerning licensing of dialysis units in eastern Ontario. I contacted my NMC associates immediately and on the day of the press conference the group came in from Boston. They, the Ottawa lawyer representing them, and I attended the press conference.

There were about twenty-five or so people present, representatives from the Kidney Foundation, the hospital, other bidders, and, of course, the press. When the minister announced that the winners were the Ottawa Carleton Dialysis Company and the Eastern Ontario Dialysis Company, I was only somewhat pleased because I thought we had won just the licence for Ottawa. When I told our lawyer, he laughed and said I'd obviously forgotten that the Eastern Ontario Dialysis Company was the name of the Cornwall clinic. So, in fact, we were approved for both.

It was very exciting, but the good feeling didn't last long.

Two days later, the leader of the official opposition stood up in the Ontario legislature and attacked the minister of health and the government for awarding the dialysis units to a Dr. Posen and an American company so corrupt that it was denounced on the front page of the *New York Times*. The minister replied that they'd not been aware of the connection between Dr. Posen and National Medical Care; if they had been they never would have awarded the licence to him. This was blatantly untrue but, because the statement was made in the legislature, we had no legal redress.

However, things turned around when, in a press scrum outside the legislature, the minister repeated his claim that he had not been informed. As soon as the words were out of his mouth in public it became libel because I had evidence that our proposal had included our association with NMC. Our document had proposed ownership by a non-for-profit corporation, and to contract with NMC to setup and run the clinics under me as medical director. I would chair the not-for-profit corporation, and representatives of NMC, the hospital, and the community would comprise the board. There was no doubt that the ministry had been informed.

The next day, the minister was attacked again in the legislature as well as in the press, this time because the units weren't awarded to a Canadian company. The minister then revoked the licences he had awarded to us.

I was being bombarded with questions from the press at my office and at home. Within twenty-four hours I'd had over twenty calls from press from across the country. Luckily, I had a medical meeting to attend in Chicago and I flew out of Ottawa figuring no one would bother me there. I was wrong. The media managed to trace me to Chicago and gave me no peace, so I took off to where no one would find me: I went home. Everyone naturally assumed that I'd gone into hiding – and I had: at home. Since it was the weekend, I had time to gather my thoughts.

On the Saturday, I received a call from my colleagues at NMC asking me to come to a meeting in Boston the next day. The meeting took place in the corporate offices of NMC. The president of the company was a nephrologist, Dr. Constatine L. Hampers, who was responsible, in large part, for establishing universal coverage for haemodialysis for all US citizens who needed it. He'd fought the government and won. Chronic kidney failure was the only disease in the US where the therapy was – and still is – covered entirely through Medicare, with no age barrier. Of all the countries in the world, the US had the highest rate of patients on haemodialysis, because everyone could be covered.

The president made me an offer I couldn't refuse. He explained, basically, that this large company would support me if I wanted to fight the Ontario government. But, he warned, it would be difficult and there was no guarantee of the outcome. He reiterated that the company would cover the financial costs, warned me, yet again, of the psychological trauma I might be facing, then left the decision to me.

I decided to accept the challenge and they arranged for one of the top lawyers in Ottawa, David Scott, to handle the case. Mr. Scott had recently acted successfully for former Prime Minister Jean Chrétien.

At a meeting with the lawyer and company representatives, it was decided to sue the minister of health for libel because, when he spoke outside the legislature, he'd said things about me that were incorrect. To show we weren't doing it for the money, we decided to sue him for a token amount plus expenses. In addition, we were demanding the government give us back the original licence. Someone also felt that I should take a one-day course on how to talk to the media. It was an excellent idea. The course was interesting and proved to be very useful.

The case eventually went to court where our lawyer, armed with the evidence, made mincemeat of the government. We won the case handily. They were ordered to pay us $30,000 and costs – about $250,000 – and to give us the licence to operate the two clinics.

While all this was happening, NMC was bought out by Fresenius Medical Care, a German multinational company.

The new president of North American operations was an American scientist who was very knowledgeable about dialysis. He'd been on a team that developed a new type of dialysis filter, which dramatically changed the way haemodialysis was performed. He was anxious to settle the government problem quickly, so he arranged for us to meet the deputy minister of health to work out a solution.

We met at Toronto's Pearson Airport and talked strategy on a limousine ride into the city. All through our strategy discussion he was on the phone talking million-dollar deals around the world. He said he wanted me to do most of the talking with the deputy minister.

Our meeting with the deputy minister went very well except the president, who had insisted that I do the talking, took over and started talking right from the beginning. It was fifteen minutes before I got an opportunity to speak. In any case, we were granted the licence. Our meeting took place in the spring – I think it was April – and we hoped to have the clinics open seven months later in November.

It was lunchtime when we left the deputy minister's office and the president suggested we get something to eat. I agreed, knowing that there were many fine restaurants in the area. However, my companion spotted a hot dog wagon so we each had a hot dog and a drink. He paid for lunch. I said, "If I'd known you were going to pay, I would have ordered fries." We became friends after that and met frequently at meetings. He always tried to urge me to develop more units in Canada, but to this day Canadian provincial governments are against anything that smells of private medicine.

As planned, our two units opened in November, 1998. They were, and still are, very successful. We were accredited by the College of Physicians and Surgeons of Ontario. The units are considered the best of the independent dialysis units. In fact, the Ontario government uses them as model units. As for the court case, I don't think we ever received either the $30,000 or the expenses.

Dr. Steven Nadler took over as medical director of the Ottawa and Cornwall clinics when I retired. Steven recently informed me that we have received full accreditation from Accreditation Canada. This is a great honor. Accreditation Canada accredits hospitals and medical facilities of all sizes, including the university hospitals. Our units are the only free-standing dialysis units in Canada to achieve that distinction.

* * *

When chronic haemodialysis was first developed, in 1962, there were few dialysis machines and funding was touch-and-go, so patient eligibility was restricted. The first patients had to be less than fifty years of age and contributing members of society (that is to say, employed or a woman with children). As more funds became available, age alone became the determining factor, but the elderly still were not accepted. That changed with advent of Medicare in the US, where all patients over age sixty-five were entitled to all medical therapy. This had a strong influence on

Canada, and now our elderly are the commonest treatment group.

The oldest patient I started was an eighty-five-year-old Ottawa Civic Hospital patient. It was 1990 and unheard of to dialyze someone that old. He was an independent gentleman who lived by himself until age ninety-two when he deteriorated and moved into a long-term care facility. He died at ninety-three.

One of our original clinic patients began at the age of seventy-nine. He had a housekeeper/companion and he liked to travel. He was from England and he wanted to go there for a holiday. I had a hard time arranging for him to be dialyzed in England because every unit I contacted said he was too old – they didn't accept patients over sixty. I finally got him into a unit outside London. After his visit, the unit wrote back to say they couldn't believe how well he was. They ultimately changed their criteria and dropped age as a factor. This gradually occurred throughout the UK and, I believe, our patient had a role in that transformation. He has gone back to England every year since that first visit and is now in his nineties, still mentally agile but fragile.

Another woman who had been on dialysis at our Cornwall clinic for five years died in her sleep at eighty. She always dressed smartly and always looked very good whenever she came for dialysis. I visited the clinic every two weeks and she always had her hair done prior to my visit. Her daughter told me her mom treated the dialysis as if it were a job, and three times a week she came to "work."

Another elderly man, also from Cornwall, had started dialysis in Ottawa at seventy-five and transferred to Cornwall when we opened the clinic. At eighty-three he developed a severe complication and required several blood transfusions. We were sure he wouldn't survive, but he did. Every Christmas he flew to Vancouver to spend the holiday with his children, but two years ago he fell and broke his hip and had to be in rehabilitation for six months. He is now reasonably well and, at ninety, talking about another trip to Vancouver this Christmas.

The eldest patient I had who underwent open-heart surgery and an aortic valve replacement was eighty-six. He sailed through the operation, was home in two weeks, and lived for another six years in reasonable health.

There are many stories of success in dialysis in older patients. As this age group grows in the general population the number of elderly dialysis patients will also grow. This is a major consideration for the funding of health care in the future.

The elderly can live an almost normal life on dialysis. The daughter of a patient who passed away after two years on dialysis couldn't thank me enough for the extra two years she had with her mother that she would not have had without dialysis.

When we first started the free-standing dialysis units we were restricted as to whom we could take. That is, we would only accept young, well patients who were stable on dialysis. We demonstrated that a patient who is well enough to be at home can be treated just as successfully in an outside clinic as in an in-hospital clinic. All our elderly and sick patients hate having to return to hospital for any treatment.

Nimkee

I was asked to see a patient on the General Medical Service who had been studied by many very competent MGH physicians, none of whom had been able to pinpoint his problem. He was a high steel worker living and working in New York. The man had severe abdominal pain and was very anemic, and also had a small amount of blood and protein in his urine.

He was in his mid-forties, a First Nations man from the Mohawk tribe. When I asked him to tell me exactly what he did for a living, he told me that for the last two or three years he'd been stripping paint off large bridges in New York. He said the foremen always urged the workers to drink the milk that was provided by the company but he couldn't drink it because it caused him stomach pains. He had also been given a mask to wear but he didn't like the feel of it so he never wore it.

It sounded to me like he might have lead poisoning. Lead is, or was, often an ingredient in paint and this man, whose job was stripping paint, didn't wear a mask when he worked. I also knew that the reason the company provided milk was because milk helps excrete lead from the body. However, since this man was obviously lactose intolerant, he didn't drink the milk, and so had no way of getting rid of the lead. Instead, it built up in his body and brought about lead poisoning, which causes stomach pain and anemia.

The only symptom I couldn't quite account for was the abnormalities that were present in his urine. However, I checked the literature and found that lead poisoning is associated with a condition similar to glomerulonephritis and, like glomerulonephritis, protein and blood show in the urine. That explained the renal abnormalities.

We measured the fellow's lead levels and found them to be very high. Fortunately, there was treatment available. He was started on it, improved rapidly, and was discharged home.

I established my reputation with that diagnosis.

Two reasons lay behind its success. First, the difficult pediatric final exam that had included a question on lead poisoning, which had not been covered during the year. I racked my brain to get the right answer to that question and getting it led to my being considered for the prize in pediatrics. Years later, having that knowledge led me to make the diagnosis many senior people missed.

The second reason was the example set by the demanding Dr. Cameron, who always insisted that his interns present very thorough case histories.

I once helped one of my fourth-year students prepare to present to Dr. Cameron. He'd studied night and day for a solid week, we drilled in all the history and he was up on the latest literature on the man's disease.

When his time came to present, the student opened by saying, "This forty-five-year-old factory worker presented with…" At that point Dr. Cameron cut him off, proceeded to go on at great length about the importance of knowing exactly what a patient did in his job, then described various jobs and how each might cause a problem or problems. When he was through lecturing, Dr. Cameron turned to the patient and asked him what he did.

The reply was, "I push a button." Although the answer was surprising, Dr. Cameron was absolutely right. (It taught us all a very valuable lesson. It was that lesson that allowed me to make the diagnosis that made me famous for a week.)

* * *

Many years later Dr. Cameron's method surfaced again when I was chief of nephrology at the Ottawa Civic Hospital. On that occasion, the head of emergency, who was from India, asked me to see his father, who had severe high blood pressure. Dad had been thoroughly investigated and no secondary cause for the problem had been found, but his son asked if I'd mind giving a third – perhaps it was even a fourth – opinion.

I examined Dad and found nothing unusual in his history or his physical. Then I vaguely remembered that there's a type of black licorice from India that can cause people with a propensity to high blood pressure to develop very high blood pressure. I asked Dad about licorice and he volunteered that he loved the stuff and ate a lot of it every day. He stopped eating the licorice and that was the end of his high blood pressure.

We all owe a great deal to our teachers. The demanding Dr. Cameron was one renowned for his relentless attention to detail, but he taught me well. I used many of the methods he taught and then taught them to my students.

~

We know now but didn't know then that aboriginal people have a high incidence of lactose intolerance. They lack the enzyme lactase that breaks down milk and milk products, which causes abdominal pain and diarrhea. In fact, lactose intolerance is so prevalent among aboriginals that they often have to stop drinking milk as soon as they're out of infancy.

The Mohawks' ability to work on bridges and high buildings is legendary and often thought to be an innate skill. Later in my career I learned the truth about this urban legend when I did a clinic in the Mohawk reserve of Akwesasne. I asked the question and the Mohawks had a good laugh. "No, we're not born with it," they said. "Each man has to be taught how to do it and learning how to do it is very scary." They said the work was extremely hard but it paid very well – and it's also a macho thing to do, which is why they dare to do it.

* * *

In the late 1970s, I had as a patient a Cree Indian chief from the Golden Lake Reserve who was in a great discomfort from complications of diabetes and renal failure. Not surprisingly, he was very depressed. In those days there were still many things we did not know how to treat and nothing we gave him seemed to help the pain. He was also quite severely nauseated.

Elaine Steen, the head nurse on the ward, was a super lady and a great nurse. She and I were often in agreement about how to treat patients, even if the treatment was a little unorthodox. So, one day when the chief said to me, "Dr. Posen, I think it would help if I could smoke a joint," I knew she'd be on side and I said, "Sure."

He had a private room because of isolation due to infections, and whenever he smoked pot his door was shut and a sign that read DO NOT DISTURB – SEVERE INFECTION was posted on it while he self-medicated to his heart's content. Later, as his general condition began to improve, he told me the marijuana really had helped; it had taken him out of his depression and relieved his pain and nausea. In fact, he was so grateful that, to show his appreciation, he wanted to make me a blood brother. I said I'd be honoured.

During the ceremony, which took place one morning in his hospital room, the chief clasped my hands in his, said some words in Cree and bestowed on me the name "Nimkee," which means "Thunder." It was quite an honor to have a native name given to me, especially in that setting.

* * *

I always had a very large referral practice involving complex kidney or high blood pressure problems. As I got closer to retirement, the referrals lessened – except for those that came from a physician, Dr. Marlen Cook, who was a Cree working in the Akwesasne reserve on Cornwall Island. She always sent interesting cases and I was very impressed with her knowledge and her wonderful way of dealing with her patients and their families.

I decided that I would like to meet her face to face instead of just discussing patients over the phone and, since I used to go to the dialysis clinic in Cornwall twice a month, we arranged to meet over lunch during one of my visits. As I anticipated, our meeting went very well. We both had a great deal of respect for each other; it was a mutual admiration society.

The aboriginal population is predisposed to distinct medical problems. Their rate of diabetes is very high, which leads to cardiac and renal problems, among others. Alcoholism, cigarette smoking, and obesity are prevalent. There are available modern medicines that will alleviate or decrease the rate of cardiac and renal disease along with high blood pressure, but drugs alone will not help the other issues.

Dr. Cook felt that if we used native ways and combined them with modern medicine we might be more successful in treating these problems. I was very excited at the idea. I had worked with First Nations communities in the north and knew the problems but, unfortunately, not the cures. We worked out a tentative plan, aware that we would have to present it to the band council, which we did. The presentation seemed to go well; there appeared to be interest on the part of the council.

I started going to Akwesasne once a month and established a renal clinic there where I saw referred patients and followed patients with kidney disease. I never heard any more about the idea of combining native and modern medicine. Then Dr. Cook quit suddenly and went to work at a reserve in the north. She was an excellent doctor and all the patients in Akwesasne missed her. I never got a chance to find out from her why she left, but the public health nurse eventually told me there had been disagreements with the council. I was disappointed; I felt we had missed an opportunity to do something unusual to perhaps help a lot of people. Dr. Cook was a Cree from northern Manitoba and, as a woman from a different tribe, the all-male Akwesasne council didn't like her trying something new.

I continued with my Akwesasne clinic for another year and then I fully retired in 2009. I liked working with the aboriginal people. The clinic staff and I did get some good results in dealing with their diets and smoking and the patients also took their medications more faithfully. I didn't change meds but just reiterated what their Cornwall doctors said. I think because they thought of me as an important person coming a distance to see them, they would try to work with me.

An interesting aside: I was friendly with all the staff and so, when the head public health nurse's son needed accommodation in Ottawa, I offered our home.

It happened this way: Phil, the nurse's son, was scheduled to enter Carleton University in September. However, it was already August, too late to get accepted into residency, and his mother was very worried about where he would live. Josée and I had had students stay with us before. We'd housed a Swedish exchange student, a Samoan student, a hockey player from North Bay, Ontario, who played with the Ottawa 67's, a nephew who stayed and went through engineering at Carleton, and a grandnephew who spent his first year at Ottawa University with us. Phil would be another welcome student in a long line of students we'd welcomed into our home.

When Phil moved in it was a bit of a cultural shock for all of us. He is a full-blooded Mohawk and very proud of his traditions; we are Jewish and keep a kosher home. We all adapted and learned a lot about each other. After first term, Phil got into residence. He was a good student and eventually went to Syracuse University on a full scholarship.

Out of Africa

In January, 1973, the Ottawa Civic Hospital was starting a new division of nephrology. Nephrology was under urology at that time. The head of urology, Dr. Ed Collins, asked if I'd consider applying for the position of chief of nephrology at the Civic. There were great problems at the Civic, not least among them that the two nephrologists didn't talk to each other and there was an epidemic of hepatitis in the dialysis unit. I was young – thirty-eight – but I thought, despite the problems, it would be worth taking the chance. Besides, in my usual cocky way, I was sure I could right the situation. I decided to apply and was offered the position. In July, 1973, I became the Civic's chief of nephrology.

I remained chief for the next thirteen years. Initially, there were just two of us; the other nephrologist left when I took over. My partner then was Dr. Shiv Jindal. We got along very well and shared the workload. After a year, I brought Dr. Eli Rabin (the same friend that visited me in jail and told the world of my problems) from Montreal to join us. I divided the main work so that Shiv was responsible for the transplant program, for which he did a great job over the years. I put Eli, who had a PhD in biochemistry, in charge of the lab and research. I took over all dialysis and administrative matters. We shared call and covered for each other as needed. We built the Civic nephrology program into a very good unit.

* * *

Soon after I became chief of nephrology I received a call from a general practitioner asking if I would see quickly an individual who had severe hypertension.

"No problem," I said.

He had to be seen right away. Again, I said, "No problem."

Then the GP added, "By the way, the man is a guerrilla fighter in Rhodesia and there's a price on his head in Africa."

"Fine."

I pictured the patient coming into the office toting a machine gun in one hand, a machete in the other, and sporting a bullet necklace. Not even close. The fellow who showed up was in his early forties, a tall, gentle, soft-spoken man with very soft eyes. His name was Edward Ndlovu and I took an immediate liking to him. He was part of Joshua Nkomo's rebels fighting against Ian Smith's regime and was also Nkomo's foreign-minister-in-exile. He had traveled the world extensively and during his travels he had been admitted to hospitals in many different countries to be treated for high blood pressure.

The day he came to me his blood pressure was sky-high – 220/140 – and he had severe signs of hypertension affecting his eyes and kidneys. If left untreated it would destroy his kidneys and lead to kidney failure, heart failure, and certain death. I admitted him to hospital on the spot, brought his blood pressure under control and put him on oral medication. He soon felt much better. His eyes improved, and his renal functions improved but still showed signs of damage. The kidneys were functioning at about 30 percent of normal but with continued good blood pressure control it would be expected to stabilize. At that level he could expect to remain normal without going into kidney failure.

Edward was married to a Canadian whom he had met through Canadian University Service Overseas (CUSO). At the time, his wife was living and working in Zambia. He remained in Ottawa for several months, staying with mutual friends from CUSO and working on various projects for Joshua Nkomo. This gave me a chance to monitor his health and stabilize his blood pressure. He was very impressed with the care he received at the Civic Hospital, and had the highest praise for the nephrology department, pronouncing it superior to any in which he'd received treatment previously, which included hospitals in England, Russia, and Germany, among others.

He had virtually no money. He lived on a small stipend from Nkomo, but I was able to obtain a year's supply of medications for him from a drug company. I can't remember what drugs we put him on, but he did quite well. I advised him to try to see somebody in Zambia when he returned there and to be certain to seek medical help wherever he went. He promised he would.

A year later he showed up again because his supply of drugs had run out. He had seen no doctors over the past year because he trusted no one. I checked him and was pleased to find things quite stable. In fact, his renal function had improved and his creatinine, although elevated, was reasonable. I got him another two-years' supply of medication and off he went.

Three years passed without contact from him. Then, one day, I received a call from someone in CUSO who explained that he was an associate of Edward Ndlovu's. Edward was not well and he was coming to see me. I assumed he'd run out of his medication, hadn't been able to renew it and very probably was in renal failure.

I was almost certain he would require dialysis, so I arranged to get him the special medical coverage for out-of-country visitors who were healthy. The operative words here were *who were healthy* – which Ndlovu definitely was not – but I figured I'd worry about how to pay for his dialysis after I got him dialyzed. I met Edward at the Ottawa airport and he looked awful. We went straight to the hospital, where I immediately got him admitted and dialyzed because he was, as I had thought, in kidney failure. Once he was on dialysis I had to deal with the issue of payment.

First, I went to the hospital administration. They were wonderful. They gave me their full approval to continue treating Edward.

In 1977, Edward Ndlovu was still Joshua Nkomo's foreign-minister-in-exile. Since Canada was supporting Nkomo by imposing sanctions on the white regime of Ian Smith in Rhodesia, I was sure the Canadian government would support his medical care. As luck had it, Mr. Nkomo was coming to Ottawa as the guest of Ed Broadbent, then leader of the left-wing NDP party in the Canadian parliament, to speak at an NDP function. He also was scheduled to meet with Prime Minister Trudeau.

I arranged to meet with Mr. Nkomo so I could explain that the only hope for Edward was a successful kidney transplant. I knew that Edward had three siblings: a sister and two brothers. If one of their tissues matched his, a transplant had a very good chance of success and Edward would be able to carry on as normal, as long as he took drugs for the rest of his life. The question: how and where to get all the tests done to determine the suitable candidate, and how to bring the suitable sibling to Ottawa to undergo the operation? And who would pay for all this and for the follow-up drugs? Mr. Nkomo had to be apprised of the situation so that we could work out how to make it happen. The problem was further complicated because the sister was in Zambia and had recently married, one brother was in Cuba training to be a guerrilla fighter, and the other was in Mozambique already fighting.

The government under Prime Minister Trudeau agreed to pay for all the required tests and therapy.

I was picked up by limo for my meeting with Mr. Nkomo and driven to the Château Laurier Hotel in downtown Ottawa, where I was met by three tough, sinister-looking bodyguards who brought me to the great man. Mr. Nkomo was in a meeting room sitting on a chair on a small stage.

Nkomo was a huge man. He was surrounded by even more Herculean bodyguards and the room was full of serious-looking Africans all wearing black suits. No one smiled. I thought, "Wow, am I in over my head here!" I couldn't guarantee the operation would be successful, and what if Edward died during the procedure?

Once the formalities were over, Mr. Nkomo and I got down to discussing the precarious state of Edward's health. I explained the gravity of his condition, strongly recommended that Edward have a kidney transplant, and told him this would necessitate finding a donor match, ideally a member of Edward's family. If we could get the three siblings' blood test results sent to me, I said, one of them would likely be a match and might be willing to donate a kidney to Edward.

Mr. Nkomo had another idea: he would bring the siblings directly to Ottawa so that I could judge more easily which was the best donor and this would save time. I was astounded. Again I had that terrible thought, "What if something goes wrong?"

But Mr. Nkomo was as intuitive as he was imposing. As if he could read my mind, he smiled and in his deep baritone voice he said, "Things don't always go as planned. And if things do not go well at least we'll know we have done the best we could for my friend Edward."

I breathed a huge sigh of relief.

The Ndlovu siblings were flown to Ottawa to undergo the tests, which indicated his sister was the best match, and she agreed to donate a kidney to her brother. After the surgery, both Edward and his sister did exceptionally well. She returned home within a week and went on to have several children. One brother returned to Mozambique. The other brother, who was an artist, received permission to stay in Canada and study in Montreal.

After he was discharged from hospital, Edward remained in Ottawa for a couple of months and had absolutely no medical problems. We obtained a three-year supply of medicine for him and asked him to be sure to see medical people closer to home on a regular basis. He never did. He always ended up coming back to see us.

On one of his visits after the surgery, Edward underwent tests that showed that he had developed protein in his urine that could be due to many things. We had to discover the cause and treat it to protect the transplanted kidney.

I did a kidney biopsy on him (that is, I put an long needle into his transplanted kidney and took a small sample) for a pathologist to study under the microscope. The biopsy showed nothing specific, so we continued on the treatment as before. Even with the protein problem, his transplanted kidney was working well. Years later he developed full-blown diabetes, and I now realize that early diabetes was the probable cause of the protein.

The next thing I heard from Edward Ndlovu was that elections were held and that Robert Mugabe and Joshua Nkomo had agreed to share power.

It was around this time that Edward developed diabetes. He was back in Zimbabwe where a very good Zimbabwean physician who was following him had diagnosed the diabetes and had him on therapy. His doctor and I talked on the phone frequently to go over Edward's medications.

Then, one day, word came through CUSO that Edward had been thrown into jail in Harare by Robert Mugabe, who took over – and still holds – total power in Zimbabwe. Apparently, Edward was imprisoned because he was a member of the opposition under Nkomo. In fact, Mugabe had put all of Nkomo's men in jail. Edward's distraught family and friends feared that he wouldn't get proper care for his diabetes and kidney problems and would die in jail.

My wife, Josée, was a senior public servant in Ottawa at the time and she had a woman working for her who was married to a Canadian senator. Through the office of then Prime Minister Brian Mulroney, the senator arranged for me to meet with the clerk and an assistant clerk of the Privy Council, the most senior civil servants in the federal government. On top of this, Lubor Zink, a patient of mine who was a columnist for the *Ottawa Sun*, wrote a column about Edward's situation that was picked up by *The Globe and Mail*.

Coincidentally, the Zimbabwean government and Robert Mugabe had asked the Canadian government for a loan of $20 million. They got the loan on the unspoken but understood condition that they release Edward Ndlovu from jail. Of the twenty colleagues arrested with him, Edward was the only one freed.

He was well for about three or four years and then, one day, he suddenly showed up in my office. He was losing weight and felt very unwell. He had seen other physicians but really only trusted me. Examination revealed a big mass in his liver. It was a cancer for which there was no treatment. I gave him a large supply of pain medication and he returned to Zimbabwe. He died there a year later.

In Bulawayo, Zimbabwe's second city, there is a main boulevard named after Edward Ndlovu.

New developments

As far back as my days as a resident, I was searching for a way to keep track of articles I'd read and patients I'd seen. I wanted to create a database that would allow me, for example, to easily access the records of all my patients. These days, with a computer on every desk, it sounds simple enough. But in the 1960s and 1970s there were only large mainframe computers that took up whole rooms. I wanted then what we have now: I dreamt of a small desktop device that I could use to set up a database.

When my wife and I visited the Ontario Science Centre, in Toronto, in 1975, two Apple computers were being demonstrated. These were very early models, before the advent of hard drive and memory. Each computer included a five-inch disc that had a disc operating system on it. The computer itself had no memory. Nonetheless, it was groundbreaking. I was very taken with it and realized it was the wave of the future. In medicine, other than by hand, there was as yet no means to compile and analyze all the data that we were accumulating. I had a punch hole system to retrieve articles I read but it was very cumbersome.

I decided I should get one of those computers and learn how to use it. So I bought an Apple II Plus for about $3,000. It had no memory, but DOS was included in the soft discs with the programs. Then I went to Algonquin College, in Ottawa, to take courses on programming and on the spreadsheet software Lotus

1–2–3, and developed my own financial spreadsheet and an early version of data retrieval for nephrology. Neither of them was very good, but I could see the potential for computer use.

At the time, I had a dialysis technician working with me by the name of Chris Crowe who was interested in computers. Chris and I decided we'd design a program for dialysis patients so we could keep track of their course. And, if we could add lab work, we should be able to analyze all things pertinent and come up with the important correlations that would help us improve patient care. I took off three months as a sabbatical to work on the project.

At some time during the sabbatical, I realized that neither Chris nor I had enough knowledge to do what we were trying to do and that the computers we were trying to use didn't have the power or memory for what we hoped to achieve. Meanwhile, I still had dreams of a medical use for the computer, so I made an appointment with the head of a large software company in Ottawa. I hoped he would be interested in having me assist a team in developing a program. As it happened, the fellow was not even vaguely interested and after a ten-minute meeting I was summarily dismissed. Over the next few years medical computing became very big. Too bad I couldn't interest that group; we could have been pioneers.

* * *

In November, 1992, I attended the annual meeting of the American Society of Nephrology in Baltimore. The ASN is the largest scientific gathering of kidney specialists in the world. The division of nephrology usually sends as many trainee nephrologists as possible. These meetings are very educational.

On the second evening, a colleague of mine, Dr. Peter Magner, and I took our three fellows at the meeting for a late dinner. At 10:00 PM, after we'd finished the meal, our guests suggested we meet up with a group of Canadian nephrologists who were going out for drinks at an Irish pub. I hesitated, explaining that I was not as young as they were – all in their twenties and early thirties. At fifty-seven, I was no longer able to stay up late and play, then get up and attend sessions the next day. Eventually they wore me down and I agreed to tag along – with the proviso that I would leave about midnight.

We arrived at the pub to be greeted by a host of colleagues from all across the country. They were having a grand old time and within minutes I was in the thick of the action and wound up drinking, talking, dancing, and singing until close to 3:00 AM. The pub was very smoky, but I was certainly no stranger to smoke and it didn't bother me. I'd been a light smoker but had quit it when I was about forty. I managed to make it to the sessions the next day but I didn't feel great. Two days later the meeting ended and I went home.

On my first morning at home I awoke with a cough and fever. I was sure it was something I'd caught in the pub or in the airplane but after two days, when I hadn't improved, I called my doctor, Deborah O'Keefe, who arranged to see me the next day.

The next morning, I awoke feeling fine. No cough. No fever. I called Deborah to say we might as well cancel the appointment but she wouldn't hear of it. "No," she said, "you're over fifty and you need a check-up anyway, so I'm expecting you." I thought, "What a waste of time!" But I obeyed and duly presented myself at the appointed hour.

Deborah examined me and, fortunately, everything was normal on the physical. She also insisted that I have a chest X-ray, and I thank God that she did. The X-ray showed a small density in the lower lobe of my left lung that was not felt to be associated with my acute bronchitis, which had gotten better.

A biopsy of the lesion showed it to be cancer.

All this transpired just before Christmas. Since the chest surgeon, Dr. Farid Shamji, is a Muslim, and I am a Jew, he arranged for the surgery to take place over the Christmas holiday, 1992.

The pre-op tests showed no evidence of spread, which was good news. At surgery the tumour was small, although the pathology from the biopsy showed a round cell malignancy, which is usually associated with a terrible outcome.

Because the tumour was small, Dr. Shamji elected to remove only the lower part of the left lung, which was where the tumour was located. But he ran into a problem: whereas in normal people the upper and lower lobes of the left lung are divided into two by a sulcus (a sort of divisional groove between lobes), Dr. Shamji discovered that I didn't have a sulcus. He decided to create one, and the procedure resulted in excessive bleeding which, thankfully, he got under control. Having lost only one lobe of one lung, I was left with sufficient lung tissue to carry on skiing and biking.

I was off work for about two months but by spring I felt well enough to return to biking – even to ride the twelve kilometres from home to work, and back.

I was very fortunate, indeed, because if I hadn't developed acute bronchitis I wouldn't have sought out my doctor and the tumour, which was very small when discovered, would probably have grown and spread, as that type of tumour is prone to do. Had that happened, by the time actual symptoms appeared it would have been inoperable.

Every six months since the surgery I have undergone routine follow-ups. For the first six years I got a clean bill of health at every appointment. Then, in the sixth year, the examination revealed a lesion on my left upper lobe. The biopsy demonstrated a squamous cell malignancy – a different type of tumour with an even worse outlook then the first.

Fortunately, this tumour, like the previous tumour, was very small. So small, in fact, that they had great problems doing the biopsy. The verdict: total removal of my left lung. The operation was difficult because there was scarring from the first operation. Post-op, I ended up in the intensive care unit for a few days.

When I woke up in the ICU, four patients that I'd been looking after prior to my own surgery were in the ICU with me. The dialysis nurse caring for the quartet was a friend who had worked with me frequently and when he came to dialyze the patients, I started giving him orders! He always smiled politely but I suspect he followed orders from the nephrologist in charge. One of the ICU nurses teasingly wondered how OHIP (the Ontario Health Insurance Plan) would feel about getting a bill from my surgeon for me, and one from me for attending my patients in the ICU when I was a patient, too.

It took a very long time for me to recover from the second operation, but I was tumour-free for twelve years. Having just one lung, I can no longer bike or ski the way I used to but, as my surgeon said, "Be grateful you're alive after bouts with two bad cancers." I am, indeed, grateful and have found other ways to enjoy my life.

I was tumour-free for twelve years.

* * *

I was very depressed after my first operation and, after I'd been off work for two months, I was convinced I'd forgotten everything I knew. My physician wisely suggested that I take a course or find a meeting to attend.

I took her advice and found a meeting in Keystone, Colorado, in the mountains west of Denver. Its focus was haemodialysis access, a topic that greatly interested me because access to blood circulation in haemodialysis is a major problem in chronic haemodialysis programs. All haemodialysis patients are attached to the artificial kidney machine by a tube that runs from a vein to the machine and then returns the blood to another vein through a different tube. The sites where we place the tubes frequently get blocked and we have to move to other sites on the body. We prefer to use the arms and, unfortunately, have to use large needles that are uncomfortable for the patients. Other methods often lead to infection and often block.

In Colorado, days were designed to allow meeting attendees an opportunity to ski the great powder snow of the Rocky Mountains. Never had I skied such great snow and such amazing mountains before. It was thrilling. The meeting was great, too. Lectures began at 7:00 AM, then we broke from 10:00 AM to 4:00 PM, and, at 4:00, there was a second three-hour program. The course was excellent and I brought back some very good ideas that changed the way we did things in Ottawa.

On the first or second evening in Keystone, I ran into a colleague, George Buffalo, an American PhD with whom I once had done some useful research on dialyzers. George confided he was working on a new, very exciting device that gave excellent access to the circulation and appeared to avoid many of the previous complications. It was very hush-hush stuff and if I was interested in getting involved I'd have to sign a confidentiality agreement. In fact, he and his team were actually looking for a Canadian centre to work with – they had secured one but needed a second – because it was very difficult to get approval from the US government for research on devices.

I was interested, so I signed the agreement. The next evening, George and his research group took me to a room where they demonstrated their project, which was very exciting, indeed. They were attempting to design a device that would simplify access to the blood circulation in haemodialysis. As I previously mentioned, access to the circulation has always been a major problem in dialysis. The alternative is to insert a tube in a large vein through the chest wall. Unfortunately, this method comes with its own set of problems as is at very high risk of causing severe infections.

George's group's device, which was surgically placed under the skin, could be needled with a blunt needle without puncturing the skin. It sounded very promising to me. I agreed to study it further and volunteered to experiment with it in my nephrology unit. When their first study ran into problems, the other Canadian unit backed out. But I still liked the device, and one of my patients also was ecstatic about it.

For the second study, the research team decided to call together a group of physicians, engineers, and researchers at the next ASN annual meeting, in 1997 in New Orleans. After analyzing the data and the problems, this group agreed that the basic idea was a good one and so, calling on the expertise of the engineers, we redesigned the device, taking into account all that we had learned in the first study.

This second study went much better, but my role was limited because it coincided with my second lung operation. On the basis of our study, the device was eventually marketed after passing US and Canadian approval. But over time, other problems such as infections developed and it was taken off the market.

Nonetheless, it was a great learning experience for me, particularly seeing how very involved the approval process was for new devices. I also learned that no matter how much work you put in, things don't always work out.

* * *

After the device was marketed and the problems surfaced, the company, which was called Vasca, went in a new direction: developing a method of dialysis that could be done in a simpler fashion and potentially be more effective than anything that had come before it.

The group asked me to sit on its medical advisory board, but I wasn't working yet because I was still recovering from my second bout with lung cancer. The company wanted to continue working with me and with The Ottawa Hospital, so I asked a colleague, Dr. Deborah Zimmerman, a brilliant young woman, if she would run the study in Ottawa. Deb agreed and we ran a few patients on the new system.

During the next four years I remained on the medical advisory board of the company, called NxStage – an offshoot of Vasca. We met outside of Boston five or six times a year. It was a very exciting time for me because the medical board was composed of very bright nephrologists and brilliant engineers.

The company is still doing very well and is currently a leading producer of machinery for home haemodialysis.

In from the cold

In 1975, I was scheduled to present the results of research by my colleague Dr. Denis Page and me on immunity and renal failure to the European Dialysis and Transplant Association at its meeting in East Berlin.

The Berlin Wall was very much in existence then, so acquiring travel documents posed a major challenge. I had to navigate through mountains of red tape to procure a visa and assorted travel documents. Despite the obstacles, I did manage to make it to the meeting, present the paper, and return home.

I thought nothing more of it at the time but, three or four years later, two gentlemen showed up unannounced at my office at the Civic and introduced themselves as Royal Canadian Mounted Police (RCMP). They were here, they said, because they understood I'd been in East Berlin in 1975 – and they needed to talk to me.

They explained that the East Germans were negotiating with the Canadian government to establish an embassy in Ottawa and, if they did open an embassy, they would probably invite me to some functions as a person who had travelled to East Berlin. Diplomats like to have ordinary Canadian citizens present among their guests at some functions. Should I receive such an invitation, the RCMP wanted me to keep my eyes and ears open and, if I noticed anything at all suspicious, to let them know.

I laughed. "You mean, you want me to be a spy?" I exclaimed. "Wait until I tell my family! My boys will be really excited when I tell them I'm going to be a spy for the Mounties." Both men turned beet red, excused themselves, and left.

The East Germans never did open an embassy here and so, fortunately, I was never put in the position of having to spy for the RCMP.

* * *

The same year, my colleague Dr. Eli Rabin and I attended a meeting in Helsinki, Finland, to present data from a research project we were working on together. Following the meeting, Eli wanted to visit Leningrad, but I refused to go to the USSR – I didn't want to spend my tourist dollars there. So I opted to explore Copenhagen. We agreed we'd spend three days touring separately and then meet up in Amsterdam.

The arrangement suited me very well because I prefer to travel alone; I like to discover a city on my own. However, there was one small problem: other than the date and time I was due back home, no one knew where I was. If someone needed to reach me I would be almost impossible to find.

When I arrived in Copenhagen, I took a cab to the centre of the city, found a beautiful old hotel, and took a room for three nights. After I dropped my luggage in the room, I walked to the nearby Tivoli Gardens where I had a lovely meal at an outdoor café and watched the world go by.

I was in a great mood after eating and people-watching and decided to take a walk along a large pedestrian mall filled with wonderful shops. As I strolled and window-shopped, I was suddenly seized with the overwhelming feeling that I should go home. I continued walking, but try as I might I just couldn't shake the feeling. Finally, unable to ignore it any longer, I went back to the hotel and arranged for a flight to Montreal the next morning. Because of the time difference, it was too late for me to call Ottawa to give my wife a heads-up that I was coming home ahead of schedule.

Part of me felt a little foolish giving in to an unsubstantiated feeling, but something even stronger propelled me onward. I felt terrible that I didn't know how to reach Eli in Leningrad; I'd just have to leave a message for him when I got home.

The next afternoon I landed in Montreal and while I was waiting for my connection to Ottawa I called home. When my wife heard my voice and heard that I was in Montreal, en route home, her relief was palpable. "Thank God," she said. "I've been trying to get you since last night." The reason for the urgency: at the very time I had been gripped by a great need to get home, my best friend, Wilf Ferguson, had died suddenly. His funeral took place the next day and I was there.

Kidney stones

Early in my nephrology career I became interested in kidney stones, their cause, and how to prevent them. However, as a nephrologist I did not treat and therefore did not see the acute cases. I had read a great deal about their presentation but the actual therapy was up to urologists.

One afternoon I was in my office at the Ottawa General when a colleague, who was head of cardiology, came in. He was in a real panic. He had blood in his urine, was sure he had acute glomerulonephritis, and was sure he was going to die. It was 1968, and chronic dialysis was just in its infancy. Many physicians still thought that chronic renal failure and haemodialysis were a death sentence.

As he was relating his symptoms he wouldn't, or couldn't, stop moving around my office. This made me suspicious. "Frank," I said, "I'm sure you have a kidney stone." He admitted to having some pain over his kidney and that the pain was getting progressively worse. I took him to emergency where he was seen by urology, given pain management and diagnosed with kidney stones. The pain from an acute renal stone is said to be as bad, if not worse, than labour pain.

Needless to say, as painful as it was, he was relieved that he didn't have acute renal failure.

* * *

Another kidney stone episode occurred in the late 1970s when I was chief of nephrology at the Ottawa Civic.

I'd been invited with my head technician, Raga Makeal, to go to Denver, Colorado, to view a new development by one of the large dialysis companies. We were supposed to spend just two days in Denver and fly home, but I had other ideas. "If I'm going to be in Denver," I said, "I want to ski in the Rockies." So, it was arranged that I would go skiing with two of the company's researchers on Saturday. They were to pick me up at 7:00 AM for the two-hour drive to Vail. We would ski all day, drive back to Denver, and I'd leave for home on Sunday morning.

Raga and I visited the research center on Friday, had a pleasant supper together, and returned to the hotel for early-to-bed. At about 11:00 at night, there was a knock on my door. I opened it to find Raga complaining of pain and unable to stop moving around. He thought he had twisted his back, but from his appearance, and after a cursory examination, I was sure he had a kidney stone.

I arranged for an ambulance and accompanied him to hospital where a physician confirmed that he had a kidney stone and gave him pain medication. When he was finally calm and stable I went back to the hotel. By then it was 4:30 AM, and I was being picked up at 7:00. There was absolutely no way I was passing up the opportunity to ski in the Rockies – so, after just two hours sleep, I got up and got ready to go.

The skiing was wonderful and more than lived up to my expectations. But then, after about two hours, when I was standing at the top of a run, I suddenly got terribly weak. I could hardly move and became very nauseated. I knew something was wrong but I didn't know what. Of course, being a macho male physician, I didn't say anything; I chalked it up to being overtired. Very slowly I inched my way to the easiest run and pointed my skis down. Somehow I made it to the bottom, removed my skis, found my way into a corner of the lodge and threw up. I spent the rest of the day in the lodge, felt better, and didn't say anything to anybody.

On the drive home when one of the associates asked if I'd had any altitude sickness, it hit me: I'd had severe altitude sickness and was very lucky nothing worse had happened. I'm sure it was due to a lack of sleep.

* * *

My first bout with my own kidney stones occurred at the end of August, 2009, on the weekend my nephew was getting married in Ottawa. All our family had come to town and was staying with us: Andy, his wife Michele, and their kids were in from New York; Dan and his wife had flown in from Barcelona, Spain; and Jacob, who had recently graduated from university – all were with us.

My wife and I were living in a two-bedroom condo. We had rented a guest suite in the building for Andy and Michele and two of their daughters. The rest of the gang was spread about our condo. At Saturday lunch there were eleven people sitting around our dining room table.

I sat down too but, strangely, I had no appetite. Then, suddenly, I desperately needed to lie down but when I did I couldn't lie still. I knew that something was very wrong. I had to break the news to everyone that I was unwell and couldn't go to the wedding, which was starting at 4:00 that afternoon.

When the pain became quite severe and went down my flank to my testis, I knew I had a kidney stone and asked Jacob to take me to the hospital.

At the hospital I received morphine intravenous and had a CT scan, which confirmed the diagnosis. Eventually the pain was controlled and I was sent home with morphine to wait it out until I passed the stone. I missed a great wedding but now know how my colleagues felt. A kidney stone is no fun. No fun at all.

* * *

The last in the unusual series of events that I am going through all started with my second kidney stone. Josée and I had just driven to Florida and the next day it was very hot and I was doing many errands. That evening before supper I developed severe pain and I knew it was another kidney stone. Josée took me to Delray Medical Center where they quickly gave me pain relief and did a CT scan to check the position and size of the stone. It was small and the physician assured me it should present no problems and I would pass it in due course; in the meantime I was to drink lots of fluids and take painkillers for relief. Then he said there was an additional problem. There was a mass in my remaining right lung that very much looked like cancer. I was overwhelmed. The physician showed me the CT scan: it looked horrible. I understood that, basically, I was finished. One cannot survive on one-quarter of a lung, so surgery was out of the question. And I was sure chemotherapy was of no help in lung cancer. I thanked the emergency physician and said it had been a great life. I returned to Ottawa the next morning and arranged to see my respirologist, Dr. Steven Bencze. He was not sure it was cancer and so I went through a series of tests with him and my chest surgeon, Dr. Farid Shamji. It turned out to be a cancer called a non–small cell adenocarcinoma in my remaining lung, three centimetres in size. Surgery was out, because I could not afford to lose more lung; radiation was also ruled out. To make it interesting, two years before, I had fallen and fractured some ribs. At emergency they did a CT scan, because the chest X-ray didn't show anything. That CT scan showed the cancerous lesion, but the report was not seen. In two years the tumour had only grown one centimetre. I then saw Dr. Wheatley-Price, an oncologist. He felt it unusual for me to have three different lung cancers, and the last so slow-growing. He did a test and discovered that I have an unusual type of tumour that occurs mainly in Asiatic women, but is responsive to one drug, called Iressa. I have been on the medication for one and a half years, the tumour has not grown, and I feel fine. I have to take one pill a day for life, and no one knows what will happen. Fortunately, the medication is covered by OHIP. It costs $30,000 per year.

At the scene

I always stop at the scene of an accident, but I have often wondered whether I was of any use at all.

The first accident that comes to mind happened when I was a staff man at the Ottawa General Hospital. We had been in Sainte-Rose, Quebec, visiting my wife's family and were now on the Autoroute heading back to Montreal to attend a wedding, when there was a massive accident just ahead of us. We didn't actually see what happened but we were on the scene before the police or ambulances arrived.

I parked my car very quickly and arranged with my wife, who was a nurse, to do triage with her. We could see that all the occupants in one car were dead; there was nothing we could do for them. From their attire, we realized they were part of a wedding party. The people in the other car were injured and bleeding. We were able to stop the bleeding and they became stable. We waited for the police and ambulances to arrive, covered with blood and devastated. We felt what we had done amounted to nothing.

Once the ambulances arrived, we went back to Sainte-Rose to change at my in-laws' home and, of course, told them the grizzly tale. The very next day relatives of the people who died in the accident called us. They'd heard we had stopped to help and wanted to express their appreciation; they wanted us to know that, despite the tragic outcome, they were comforted by the fact that whatever could be done had been done. In one of those strange twists of fate, the people who perished were friends of my in-laws.

* * *

The next event occurred when I was chief of nephrology.

During summer months I always enjoyed bicycling to and from the hospital and, one day, as I was cycling on a path along the Rideau River, I noticed a crowd gathered on the road and a motorcycle lying on the ground. I jumped off my bike, rushed over and announced that I was a doctor. The woman holding the biker's head looked up and said she was a doctor. Then another bicyclist came over to say that he was a doctor, and then another cyclist arrived and said she was a nurse. At that point everything seemed under control. There were two GPs, a nephrologist, a nurse, and more healthcare people stopping all the time. I quietly left. Fortunately, the cyclist did better than his machine.

* * *

Not long ago, Josée and I were on board an airplane bound for Portugal when the loudspeaker suddenly came on with the query, "Is there a doctor on board?" I immediately got up and was directed to a twenty-year-old who was very confused. Another doctor, a general practitioner from a small town, had also answered the call, so while he did the examination I went through the patient's wallet and discovered that he was a diabetic.

I knew that first we had to rule out hypoglycemia due to extra insulin, and the only way to do this was to give the patient IV glucose. The flight attendant brought out the medical kit containing the 50-percent glucose solution that is always used to treat diabetic coma due to insulin. The young man was very restless and, between his illness and the motion of the plane, we had a hard time holding him still. Eventually I got the needle and syringe into a vein and injected the glucose. He woke up gradually, calmed down, and was fine for the rest of the trip.

* * *

Over the many years I practiced medicine, I often had help from prominent politicians.

When we first came to Ottawa, somehow we met John Turner, at the time newly elected to the federal parliament. Mr. Turner subsequently ran against Pierre Trudeau for the leadership of the Liberal Party and lost, although he did serve as prime minister for a short time. Mr. Turner and I talked and, as we did, I found myself quite impressed with him. John Turner felt strongly, as a representative of a riding, that he had an obligation to help his constituents in any dealings with the government.

In the early 1970s, another politician, Walter Baker, came to the aid of a patient of mine. The man, who was from Trinidad, had developed chronic renal failure while here on a limited visa and required chronic haemodialysis. Ultimately, his visa ran out and he was being deported to Trinidad. At the time there were no dialysis facilities in Trinidad or anywhere else in the Caribbean. I turned to our member of parliament, Walter Baker, for help, and he was wonderful. He very quickly realized that sending the patient back to Trinidad was a death sentence and arranged for him to stay in Canada permanently.

* * *

When I was having problems with Edward Ndlovu, my Zimbabwean patient, a senator cleared the way for me to meet with people from the Department of Foreign Affairs and they were able to clear the way for Mr. Ndlovu to get the treatment he needed.

* * *

Recently, one of our fellows from India could not get his wife and infant son into Canada because the child had a problem. I spoke to Minister of Justice John Manley, who helped him get through the red tape. The fellow is now a respected nephrologist on the staff of The Ottawa Hospital doing wonderful clinical research and teaching. His son is fine.

A walk down memory lane

One Wednesday afternoon stands out as singularly memorable, a non-stop walk down memory lane.

It began when a woman who looked vaguely familiar came up and said, "Dr. Posen! I haven't seen you since dialysis camp." Twenty-three years ago I had volunteered to be the doctor at a camp for dialysis patients. "Do you remember my husband?" she asked, just as her husband came around the corner. I did indeed.

I had begun looking after the gentleman thirty years earlier and had followed him up to the time of his second transplant ten years ago. He was a wonderful man, a perpetual optimist. He went through many severe crises when he was on dialysis and with the first transplant that had failed. A second transplant was successful. Now he was in his sixties and had developed diabetes. The disease had caused foot problems and he was being admitted for amputation. But he had the same warm smile and cheerful demeanour I remembered. He greeted me warmly and thanked me profusely for all my help over the years.

* * *

Fifteen minutes later another gentleman appeared at the desk and said, "Dr. Posen! Good to see you volunteering! I'd heard that you'd retired." Initially, I didn't recognize him but he, too, was an individual who had gone through two transplants and had run into many complications from the first one. I'd worked hard with all the team to help him through that time. He'd had a second transplant fourteen years ago, all was well, and he looked great. I was very pleased to see how well these two patients had done and how they had defied the odds against dying for more than twenty years.

* * *

A little while later an elderly man asked for the room number of patient Agostino Monteduro. I recognized the name because Mr. Monteduro was a longstanding patient of mine.

I'd first seen him in 1983 when he was transferred to me from another hospital. He was in severe kidney failure and very close to death. He survived, but his kidneys didn't improve and he had to be put on dialysis. He eventually had a kidney transplant, which gave out after six years and once again he had to be short-listed to undergo a second transplant. We became friends and, in fact, he insisted on loaning me a villa in the south of Italy for a month. His family in Italy was very welcoming to my wife and me.

Agostino was very grateful for the medical care he'd received. He was very active in the Italian community and he decided to organize an Italian Night Dinner to raise funds for kidney research. The first dinner was such a success that it became an annual event in Ottawa, which I always attended. To date it has raised over $800,000 for kidney research.

I'll never forget the 1990 Italian Night Dinner. I was at the dinner, but I was also on call at the Civic that night. Agostino was on the transplant list and the nephrology department had outfitted him with a buzzer in case of a match. The transplant coordinator was there, too. Right in the middle of dinner each of us was alerted that a kidney had come available. What a moment!

Agostino had organized and coordinated the entire evening; the dinner was his baby. When he got the buzz and we told him he had to leave with me and get to the hospital immediately, Agostino got very excited and ran to the microphone to share his good news. The renowned opera singer Maureen Forrester, who was the featured entertainer that evening, announced that she would be dedicating all her songs to him. It was a very emotional moment. We left quickly, he had the transplant, and this time it was successful.

But on that memorable Wednesday afternoon when I was manning the information booth, Agostino was not at the hospital for a geriatric assessment. He was eighty-one, his wife had died suddenly, and he was trying to arrange long-term care. I went to see him, of course, and we hugged and tears flowed.

*   *   *

I returned to the desk from my visit with Angelo just in time to see three nurse managers emerge from a meeting. One of them looked over at me and, in that instant, we both recognized each other. She ran over and embraced me.

She is aboriginal and, when I first saw her, she was a student nurse and having some difficulties. I helped her get through that rough time. I followed her progress for a few years, watched her graduate, and then lost contact with her. It turned out that she had traveled, eventually found her way back to Ottawa, and was now an assistant manager in emergency. She was absolutely fine and as beautiful as ever, and makes sure that I am treated special when I go to the emergency room.

* * *

The final surprise of the day was seeing Jay Lynch. Jay was in charge of telemedicine for The Ottawa Hospital and he and I had worked together about four years previously when I initiated the telemedicine clinic.

The telemedicine clinic connected The Ottawa Hospital to the Cornwall Community Hospital. Jay and I set up the clinic between Cornwall and Ottawa and ran into a lot of problems getting it set up.

The idea was that patients in Cornwall could come to a room in the Cornwall Community Hospital that was outfitted with a television monitor and a video camera and, simultaneously, I would be in a room at The Ottawa Hospital set up with the same equipment. Via this hookup I could see and talk to my patients in Cornwall and they could see and talk to me. All this by appointment, of course.

In nephrology, the important checks are weight, blood pressure, and observing changes in the patient's blood work. So, a few days before an appointment, the patients would get their blood work done in a Cornwall lab. We had a nurse in Cornwall who did a spectacular job. She would call patients the day before their appointment, take a little history, and apprise me of any new problems. On appointment day, prior to my seeing the patient, the nurse would take their weight and blood pressure, then fax the labs and clinical data to me so that when I saw the patient I had all the pertinent facts.

The patients loved not having to drive to Ottawa. No more fighting traffic – people from small towns always felt overwhelmed by Ottawa traffic and occasionally got lost, especially the elderly – and no more looking and shelling out for parking.

Once Jay and I got the system up and running it was so good that the patients felt totally at ease. I arranged fifteen- to twenty-minute appointments for each patient, so it was very relaxed. Since the nurse had provided me with all the patients' clinical data, blood work, and an up-to-date history concerning anything new, there were rarely any surprises. After going over any problems and settling on the therapy, we often talked about different things such as politics, sports, and family. A spouse usually accompanied the patient to the appointment. For those patients with hearing problems we communicated by telephone while simultaneously watching each other over the TV. Most of them really liked being on TV and some even said I should have been a movie star. I think the reception at their end couldn't have been very good!

Actually, the reception was excellent both ways. The nurse in Cornwall could zoom in to a specific lesion, for example an ulcer on the leg or swelling in the feet. She also listened to their lungs and could alert me to problems. She checked their pulses and cardiac rhythms. If a patient's situation became complicated or if a patient became ill, we transferred them to the care of the Ottawa Nephrology Clinic and, of course, their records were already there.

For two years – 2007 to 2009 – I was the only nephrologist in Ottawa using the program and feared it would die when I retired. I needn't have worried: when Jay spotted me at the information desk he came over to tell me I'd left a legacy. Almost every one of The Ottawa Hospital's eighteen nephrologists were now using the system. It was the largest telemedicine clinic at The Ottawa Hospital and probably in Ontario. After Jay left I was two feet off the ground, so pleased that all that effort between us had worked so well for patients. I am including two emails, one from me and a reply from Jay.

Hi Jay,

You really made my day yesterday. I had thought there was very little interest in the group for the clinic.

I was truly delighted to hear you say that I left a legacy and it has become the most used clinic. We worked hard together, it could not have happened without your support.

Thanks again.

Jerry

~

Kind thanks Dr. Posen but it was you that blazed the trail.

The Nephrology program is one of our success stories in telemedicine.

Almost every Nephrologist in the group now sees [patients] by telemedicine.

This is definitely unprecedented at [The Ottawa Hospital] – and I believe at other large academic health sciences centers in Ontario as well.

PS – You are very kind to come back to TOH as a volunteer.

Kind regards,

Jay

Jay Lynch, RN, BAdm, MSc, MEd
Clinical Telemedicine Program Coordinator
Acting Manager – AV Services
The Ottawa Hospital

* * *

All in all it was a gratifying Wednesday afternoon.

Envoi

As I write this, I consider myself to be very fortunate. I loved my profession. I was involved in nephrology very early on and was part of the early development of dialysis: haemo-, peritoneal- and home-. I was also involved with early kidney transplantation.

I had a good life with my families and children and grandchildren. I have told many of these stories to colleagues, students, and residents. They have suggested I put them on paper, so I have. In many ways these stories mirror the development of Canadian nephrology.

Dr. Posen leaving the nurses' station, Fort Resolution, Northwest Territories, 1969

Dr. Posen at the Ottawa Carleton Dialysis Clinic, 2009